THE ONLY WAY
TO SAVE AMERICA

THE ONLY WAY TO SAVE AMERICA

Trump 2.0

THE BATTLE FOR COMMON SENSE

By
Dr. Michael J. Schwartz

Published by Dead Red Media, LLC

979-8-9886132-5-1 Hardcover
979-8-9886132-6-8 Paperback
979-8-9886132-7-5 e-book

Cover design by Fiver / marmarko78

Cover illustration by Fiver / marmarko 78

Edited by Paul Blane

Formatted by Fiver / marmarko78

Printed in the United States of America

Dedication

This book is dedicated to my stepson Jaiden Sattler. We thought we had lost you in your teens when the "woke mind virus" started to infiltrate your brain. Your friends who surrounded you in high school and the mainstream media all had a detrimental effect on your thought process mold. It wasn't until you started paying attention and became awake to reality, policy, and spin that you took the leap to stick your neck out for what was right. We always knew you were smarter than the other kids around you! It takes courage to say the opposite of what everyone else is screaming when you know their screams are just noise, but that noise often drowns you out. It takes resilience to keep going back, day after day, when all they want to do is shut you down and cancel you. It takes patience to endure the weeks, months, and sometimes years before everyone else catches up with your IQ level. It takes persistence and dedication to keep moving forward in a world that seems to be falling apart around you. Most of all, it takes heart and belief that your efforts won't be in vain and that you WILL make a difference, no matter how small or to what group of people. The only thing that really matters is that you stay true to yourself in life! Do what you say and say what you do... Everyone around you is going to tell you "It's all about who you know." They just haven't figured it out yet. The secret is, it's not who you know, it's who knows you! Make sure, when people get to know you, they know you've got some balls!

CONTENTS

INTRODUCTION

TOO OFTEN, I FIND MYSELF REPEATING the same points. Whether I'm hosting my own program or appearing as a guest on someone else's, the same topics inevitably come up. The audience raises issues that lead to discussions on taxes, term limits, or education, and I catch myself saying things like, "We just talked about this last week!" It feels like we're stuck in a cycle—facing the same problems but never implementing practical, commonsense solutions.

I grew up in the United States and love my country deeply. Some might label me a nationalist, which, by definition, means I prioritize America's interests first. I see nothing wrong with that. After all, I live and work here, my family is here, and my allegiance is to this nation. Yet, there's a growing segment of people who react negatively to the idea of nationalism. They argue that we should focus more on global concerns rather than prioritizing our own country, where we work and live. This mindset, in my view, has contributed greatly to America's decline.

Now, with Donald J. Trump serving a second term as President of the United States, we have an opportunity to address many of the problems created by previous administrations. In this book, I'll share straightforward, fundamental ideas that could truly save this country. These ideas aren't controversial; in fact, the vast majority of Americans support them. So why has the government been so resistant to change? After all, we're supposed to be a government "of the people, by the people, and for the people," aren't we?

Perhaps the so-called "deep state" has been steering the ship all along, and we've simply been passengers on their ride. Of course, I'm speaking of the entrenched, unelected network of bureaucrats, intelligence officials, military leaders, and other government insiders who operate independently of elected officials to influence policy, maintain power, and resist significant political change.

The term is commonly used to describe a system where career bureaucrats, intelligence agencies, and other institutional forces act in their own interest, shaping policy decisions regardless of who holds elected office. This can manifest through slow-walking policies, leaking information to the media, coordinating opposition, or leveraging institutional inertia to maintain the status quo.

While some see the "deep state" as a conspiracy theory, others argue it is simply the natural result of a massive, entrenched government bureaucracy that prioritizes self-preservation over the will of the people.

But this moment in history may be our first real chance to expose the "deep state," reclaim our country, and chart a new course that ensures the American experiment thrives for generations to come.

THE CHALLENGE OF PRESERVATION

"A Republic, If You Can Keep It"

WHEN BENJAMIN FRANKLIN EXITED THE CONSTITUTIONAL Convention in 1787, he was asked what kind of government had been created. His response—**"A republic, if you can keep it"**—was both a confirmation of the nation's founding principles and a warning about the fragility of self-governance.

A republic is not self-sustaining. It demands an engaged and informed citizenry willing to hold leaders accountable, protect individual liberties, and resist the slow creep of government overreach. Without vigilance, the very mechanisms that uphold a republic—free elections, constitutional law, and personal freedoms—erode under the weight of corruption, apathy, and expanding bureaucracy.

Today, many of the foundational principles of our republic are under attack. **Election integrity** is questioned as processes become more complex and less transparent. **Spending is out of control**, driving national debt to unsustainable levels. **The administrative state grows unchecked**, diluting the power of elected representatives and placing control in the hands of unelected bureaucrats. Meanwhile, **the American taxpayer is increasingly burdened with an unfair and bloated tax system that punishes productivity rather than rewarding it.** These trends threaten to transform our republic into something unrecognizable, something less accountable to the people it was meant to serve.

So how do we keep the republic?

1. **Demand Transparency and Accountability** –
   Whether in elections, budgeting, or lawmaking, the
   American people must demand clarity in government
   actions. Paper ballots, voter ID laws, and single-day
   elections ensure trust in the electoral process. Zero-
   baseline budgeting forces politicians to justify every
   dollar spent rather than assuming endless growth.

2. **Reduce Government Overreach** – The Founders designed a system of checks and balances, not a bureaucratic machine designed to regulate every aspect of
   life. Reducing the size of government, particularly the
   administrative state, restores power to elected officials
   who are directly accountable to the people.

3. **Fix the Broken Tax System** – The current U.S. tax
   structure is **a convoluted, punitive disaster**. Ordinary
   Americans and small businesses shoulder the weight
   of excessive taxation, while loopholes and special interests allow large corporations and the politically
   connected to navigate the system in their favor. This
   system discourages hard work and economic growth.
   A republic cannot thrive under a government that taxes its people into submission. **Simplification, lower
   rates, and a fair tax structure are necessary to restore financial freedom and prosperity.**

4. **Defend the Constitution** – The Constitution is not a
   "living document" meant to be reshaped by unelected
   judges or political whims. It is the bedrock of American
   governance, designed to limit federal power and protect individual rights. Any attempts to sidestep or re-
   write its principles must be met with fierce resistance.

5. **Educate and Engage** – A disengaged and uninformed
   public is the greatest threat to a republic. Civics

education must be restored to its rightful place, and citizens must take responsibility for understanding their rights and responsibilities. Knowledgeable voters make better choices, and engaged citizens hold leaders accountable.

Franklin's warning was not about the immediate collapse of the republic but rather its gradual erosion if left unprotected. The responsibility to keep the republic falls to each generation. If we fail to act, we may wake up one day to find that we no longer live in a republic at all—but in something far less free.

1

A MANDATE STARTS THE CLOCK

NOVEMBER 5, 2024, WAS A HISTORIC day for the United States of America. Donald J. Trump was re-elected President of the United States, and while his detractors may not be happy, they can't ignore the historical significance of this election. The metrics of the 2024 Presidential election speak for themselves.

1. **Non-Consecutive Terms:** Trump became the second U.S. president to serve non-consecutive terms, following Grover Cleveland's presidencies in 1885–1889 and 1893–1897.

2. **Popular Vote Achievement:** He secured the highest popular vote count for any Republican presidential candidate in history, with almost 76 million votes, surpassing his 2020 total of 74.22 million.

3. **Republican Control of Government:** The 2024 election resulted in Republicans gaining control of the White House, Senate, and House of Representatives, providing the GOP with the ability to implement their agenda with minimal opposition.

4. **Demographic Shifts:** Trump made unprecedented gains among Michigan's Middle Eastern and Muslim voters; a demographic traditionally loyal to Democrats. He won 43% of votes in Dearborn, Michigan, a city known for its substantial Muslim population.

5. **Legal and Political Challenges:** Despite facing multiple legal challenges, including federal charges of election interference and a conviction in May 2024, Trump managed a political comeback, highlighting his resilience and the complexities of American democracy.

As a commentator and show host, this campaign was both fun and interesting to cover, yet the experience made me realize the fragility of our country. We witnessed two assassination attempts on Donald Trump and heard about several others that thankfully never materialized. The progressives latched onto just about anything they could, such as including Project 2025 and trying to tie Trump to jokes independent comedians were telling on stage. The ploys didn't work, and Middle America finally woke up to express their disdain for the Biden Harris policies that have economically ruined our country.

This turnaround in Middle America was driven by the fact that, to quote Tip O'Neill, former Speaker of the House, "all politics is local." When energy prices go up and individuals and companies are paying more at the pump, it affects everyone right where it hurts, their wallets. When grocery prices skyrocket and you can't afford to run your household, you tend to ignore talk about some program like Project 2025 that Donald Trump has clearly disavowed, or some joke a comedian told on stage.

What drives me nuts is the lack of intelligence evident throughout most of America. I get in trouble all the time for my opinions, and people tell me the American people are smarter than I give them credit for. I come back with, "No, they are actually dumber." I evidence that statement with the fact that America's national debt, at the time of writing, is over $36 trillion and increases by $1 trillion roughly every 100 days. It's also important to note that almost the entire country clamors for term limits, yet we keep electing the same politicians who won't vote for the measure. We have an 18% approval rating for Congress, and gridlock isn't just something that happens at rush hour. On top of that, we run our government as if the store is going out of business, and we are deliberately trying to run it into the ground for a tax deduction.

American voters have short attention spans, and they get emotional about people they don't know and have never met. They use words like, "I hate that guy" when referencing a politician, even when their only exposure to them comes in the form of a soundbite from a television interview or the opinion of a media pundit on their favorite news network. The 24-hour news cycle and politics permeate into every corner of our lives. And, at the end of the day, it's collectively our own fault.

This is meant to be a government of the people, by the people and for the people. Well, it sure doesn't work for the people anymore, and I'm hoping President Trump can change that. If past is prologue, history will tell you that Donald J. Trump does exactly what he says he's going to do, and he works hard to keep his promises. Once he's vocalized his thoughts, he acts on a duty to his family, his colleagues, and more importantly, his country to turn his visions into reality.

It's time we stopped putting band-aids on our country's gushing wounds. It's time our elected leaders stopped compromising with the other side just to gain favor on the next bill or pet project in someone's district. It's about time we apply a real tourniquet to our wounds, stop the bleeding once and for all, and fix this mess we have created. I believe Donald J. Trump is the perfect person and in the perfect position to achieve this goal. Think about it, the man doesn't care about a second term. He's got one last chance to save America once and for all.

He's got a four-year term ahead of him, and the clock started ticking the moment the election was called. From his cabinet picks to the positive signals from Wall Street the moment he was elected, they all tell you a little bit about the direction the country is headed. We need to stand with this man and fix this for ourselves, our kids, and generations to come.

I was concerned that we had lost our way, that the country I grew up in no longer existed and that those who came after me on this planet would never know the freedoms I have experienced in my lifetime. I have seen those freedoms erode throughout the decades, and as I sit here and opine, I think most Americans don't realize that their fundamental freedoms have been slipping away. In fact, ever since the government was formed in the late 1700s, our rights have been diminishing ever so slowly, at a rate which isn't always noticeable in a short 80-year life span. Our rights have been systematically chipped away at, as the behemoth of the Federal Government and its army of bureaucrats' focus has been on feeding the monster they have become. Money, power, and control would be the first three words of the constitution if it were written today—because that is what our government is based on.

When Donald Trump secured a victory on November 5, 2024, the clock started ticking. The American public is fickle, and the trend always goes against the incumbent. My estimation is that he and his team only have about 18 to 24 months before the pendulum starts swinging in the other direction. There are some races in the next two US Senate cycles that favor the Republican Party, but without both houses of Congress, it will be very difficult to get anything passed into law. We have that opportunity right now, but it may not last long. We have one chance to save America and enact measures that can put the country back on track, and in my opinion, Donald Trump is the best person to accomplish this.

For the first time in my adult lifetime, I am excited about what could be. The thing is, a lot of what could be, already once was, we just don't realize it. When we don't know our own history, we are unlikely to have a clear vision for our future. The United States was founded on many dynamic principles laid out in the Constitution, and a conservative person looks towards that document for guidance. Sadly, we have 'progressed' away from that document, ever so slowly, but the changes implemented have brought us further and further from the clear vision the founders of this country had for us all.

I've always said that if a candidate had my back on two specific issues, he or she would have my vote for life. My push button issues happen to be the abolition of income tax and term limits for members of Congress. However, the American public faces a multitude of issues as a result of all the mismanagement we have seen from both parties over the nation's history. Donald Trump not only checked those two boxes for me, but the wealth of knowledge he has gained as a businessman and by being the President previously gives him a unique perspective no other candidate brought to the table.

We have what might be a once-in-a-lifetime opportunity to protect the values of our Constitution for the future of our country and the sake of all Americans. The progressive left either doesn't understand this, or worse, does understand it and simply wants to change the fundamental structure of our Republic. The left will always have roughly 40% of the populace that goes along with whatever narrative they are being touted. And the right will continuously see roughly 40% of the vote as well. It's the middle 20% that determines the outcome of national elections—but those are the people I'm most worried about. They tend to be easily swayed and often don't understand the intricacies of the issues—people who tell you they would like to watch a Presidential debate before making up their minds. Really? They may say things like, "I vote for the person, not policy," or "character means more to me than anything else." The middle doesn't have a grasp of the issues, and you just never know what to expect from them.

According to USAFACTS, as of September 2024, approximately 186.5 million Americans were registered to vote. Among these registered voters, 45.1 million are registered Democrats, 36 million are registered Republicans, and the remaining 105.4 million are either registered with other parties or have no party affiliation. Given that the total U.S. population is about 331 million, this means that approximately 13.6% of the population is registered as Democrats, 10.9% as Republicans, and 31.8% are registered voters with other affiliations or none. It's important to note that not all states require voters to declare a party affiliation upon registration, and some states do not report these figures publicly. Therefore, these numbers are based on available data and may not capture the full picture of party affiliation across the entire U.S. population.

With that said, have you ever seen one of those interviews where random people on the street are asked questions about candidates or policy? Most of what you see on these television segments are ridiculous and embarrassing answers. Tragically, the average American doesn't understand how the government works, nor the intricacies of how the different branches of government function. They barely know who their leaders are! I can't blame them, since most Americans struggle to keep their households afloat, so it's no wonder they don't have the time to study civics. In my opinion, a person who doesn't know what they are voting for shouldn't be voting, as they show up at the polls and all too often vote for the exact opposite of what their real beliefs are.

It's a real shame that the majority of holiday dinner conversations now seem to revolve around the frustrations that our own government causes, whether it's student loans or taxes or the price of gas and groceries. I've always wanted a government so small that I don't even know if it's there. I want my family conversations to revolve around our lives and hopes, our dreams and aspirations, and I never thought Thanksgiving dinner would devolve into family members later blocking each other on social media and being uninvited to Christmas dinner. But that's what we have created by allowing our own government to run amok.

These days, politics dominates the conversation wherever you look. I think it's great that people want to get involved, and I have always encouraged everyone I know, regardless of party affiliation, to go out and vote. What kills me is when I hear someone talking about a candidate but clearly has it wrong. They have been consciously misinformed, often by the news outlet they place their trust in to give a true account about the state of the world. There were a lot of 'mistruths' told about Donald Trump during the election. But with minimal research, you'll find that a lot of those 'mistruths' were blatant, nefarious lies. Those of you who seek out alternative media sources already know this, but the majority of voters who gravitate towards the mainstream media may as well be living under a rock. The sad fact is, the moment these uninformed voters get called out on their logic and knowledge, they resort to calling Trump supporters names like Hitler and fascist. Ask them to define a fascist, and they run away. They don't see that resorting to name-calling when their reasoning doesn't hold up, actually works against their arguments, they are yelling at people who have a lot of it figured out. They are preaching to those of us who "got it" a long time ago. We have forgotten more than they'll ever know, and we're ten steps ahead of them already.

It's a shame because we're not only fighting for *our* rights and values, but we are fighting for *theirs* too! They are always the "opposite" of what they claim to be, and it's the oldest trick in their book. They call their opponents what they themselves are, and then have their opponents defend those positions. The book I'm referencing is *Rules for Radicals* by Saul Alinsky, and it says this in a little bit of a different way. It states:

> *"Make the enemy live up to their own book of rules. You can kill them with this, for they can no more obey their own rules than the Christian church can live up to Christianity."*

This tactic encourages activists to exploit perceived contradictions or flaws in their opponent's positions, forcing them into a defensive posture. Alinsky also discusses the concept of personalizing attacks, stating:

> *"Pick the target, freeze it, personalize it, and polarize it."*

This involves focusing on a specific individual or entity to make the conflict more emotionally charged and easier to address. Yes, they have a playbook that governs their behavior, and its focus is on manipulation rather than education! The conservative side is always trying to explain their policies, and the left knows, "when you're explaining, you're losing." A prevalent tactic of the democrats is to pander to people with lower education, people who they can fire up through propaganda designed to elicit an emotional response, those who can't comprehend the dynamics of an issue. They know that people make decisions when they are angry and haven't fully thought things through, and these decisions can be easily manipulated. You wouldn't trust one of these people to run your company, or even balance your personal checkbook, so why do they have such power over how we run our nation?

Honestly, I've given up on the percentage of the country that always votes left no matter the circumstances, but I haven't given up on the middle, and more importantly, the people who are intuitively on our side who may just need a little encouragement. The middle may have some sense left in them. The steep rise in gas and grocery prices may be enough to have woken them up a bit. My fear is that, after catching a glimpse of the stark reality that is America today, they might just go right back to their noncommittal ideologies once the media starts beating up logic again and the pendulum starts to swing back.

If you are on the left and happen to pick up this book, I hope you find the content helpful and illuminating. This is not an attack on your beliefs, but a respectful request to be open and reexamine your beliefs. First, you would need to put aside, temporarily, just about everything you've heard in the mainstream media. The second thing to do is speak with someone you respect but who holds different political beliefs. I know that can be difficult, but enlightenment comes from listening to other viewpoints. Just talk to your neighbors, they're not crazy, they're passionate.

In my travels, I've met a lot of patriots who've felt like me, like the government has abandoned them. More than that, they feel that the government is actively working against them. They're not wrong... Just after Hurricane Helene ravaged parts of North Carolina, residents were up in arms after revelations surfaced that FEMA workers purposely avoided households with Trump signs on their properties. The frustrations with the government are real, and that should scare anyone, no matter what side of the aisle you are on.

I met a man whose life mission was to bring these government atrocities to the forefront and fight for the betterment of the country. His name is George Colella, and he's the president of a political motorcycle club called Born to Ride for 45. George runs a group with more than 14,000 members around the country, and those members are true patriots. President Trump loves him, and why wouldn't he? After all, George has been riding around the country just to promote the Trump agenda and let other Americans know that Donald Trump has a posse to back him up. George is retired and got frustrated with the way our country was being run. He and his group are some amazing individuals who have no motive other than keeping our country safe and levelling the playing field for all Americans, regardless of party affiliation. He's supremely confident that Donald J. Trump can do that, and a lot of Americans agree!

I bring this up because Donald Trump's candidacy was unlike that of any other American President. Groups like Born to Ride for 45 wouldn't exist unless the sentiment in the country had gotten so bad that it forced everyday Americans to band together to fight behind one man for the sake of our freedoms. George is a true patriot, and I reference him because his group is a token of millions of Americans who feel the same exact way. George and I have become good friends, he was a guest at my wedding. His group doesn't waiver when it comes to protecting our rights and freedoms, and I hope those of you who are wavering or still afraid to come out and support what President Trump represents realize that the media will never show you groups like Born to Ride for 45 because they don't want you to know that Middle America is upset.

I witness this daily in the streaming shows I host. I especially enjoy hosting a streaming show because of the real-time interaction with my audience. These are everyday people from all over America, sharing their honest thoughts without any agenda beyond the safety and prosperity of their families. They aren't media pundits paid to push narratives, promote books, or regurgitate talking points. These individuals are the backbone of society, yet they are often the most overlooked. That's why they gravitate to shows like mine—to express their opinions and get immediate feedback, they are tired of shouting in frustration at the mainstream news on their TVs or radios.

Only around 6% of U.S. adults regularly obtain news from alternative social media platforms such as Rumble, Telegram, and Truth Social. About 20% of Americans get their news from social media influencers. Additionally, a significant portion of the population relies on social media platforms for news, with 54% of U.S. adults reporting they get news at least sometimes from these sources. The movement toward alternative media is growing, but old habits are hard to break. According to the Associated Press, as of October 2023, 50% of U.S. adults reported always or frequently getting election news from national news outlets, which include mainstream television networks. These mainstream media networks have often been referred to as "fake news" by President Trump, and with very good reason. Too often, they cherry-pick their items to meet their agendas, and they consciously misrepresent the facts, leaving out vital information that would leave their audiences better informed. Recent studies indicate that a significant portion of U.S. journalists identify as liberal or align with the Democratic Party. The 2022 American Journalist Study found that 50.4% of journalists identified as Democrats, marking the third-highest percentage since 1971. In contrast, only 3.4% identified as Republicans, a notable decline from 18% in 2002 and 7.1% in 2013. If consumers of mainstream media fail to acknowledge its bias, the political affiliations of these outlets should make the inherent favoritism behind their narratives unmistakable.

These media outlets focus solely on their target demographics, it's not worth their while to pander to those with differing perspectives, they know their market, and they adjust to their tastes. But a truly free press should not be rooted in the opinions of its readership. The result is, these outlets rarely address issues that impact the broader population, they prioritize stories that appeal to their established audience, ensuring their revenue streams remain steady. This approach has alienated an increasing number of everyday Americans who are frustrated by the pervasive bias and are desperate for balanced, fact-based coverage. People are weary of Thanksgiving dinner arguments with family members who have been misled by incomplete narratives, and who lack the depth of knowledge to engage in debates with peers, so they rely on rhetorical talking points rather than factual information. The core issues that impact us all rarely receive the attention they deserve, as intentional distractions, whether motivated by commercial revenue streams or political affiliation, are used to divert collective focus away from the real problems we face.

For the sake of George Colella, the good folks of Born to Ride for 45, my viewers, and the millions of Americans who've felt like this country has lost its way, it's time we discussed real issues and put real solutions on the table once and for all. It's time we started to educate not only ourselves, but those in the middle, those who are instinctively on our side but need a little handholding and guidance.

We are failing the founders of this great country because we fail to talk about the basic issues that affect all of us as a result of the distractions the media and our career politicians' wave in our collective faces. It's time to start putting those issues into perspective and making them a priority for the future of this great nation.

This book offers perspective on real issues. We're not going to discuss social issues because, in my opinion, they don't run the country. In fact, they are a giant distraction that the left has latched onto to keep your eyes off the prize. This book isn't for one-issue voters. Sadly, they are too short-sighted and will never truly understand the complexity of how our government functions. This work is for the forgotten voter, the voter, like you, who feels like a large segment of the country is ignoring them. This book is for the frustrated and disenfranchised. This book is for the silent majority of patriots who not only want to be heard but want common-sense fixes to put to bed those Thanksgiving dinner arguments we are tired of having. We need to keep our eye on the ball and protect our rights and freedoms. We've got one chance to get this right and one chance to save America. It may be *The Only Way to Save America!*

2

A NEW TAX SYSTEM

THE TRUMP ADMINISTRATION HAS INDICATED INTEREST in eliminating income tax. Obviously, no one wants the government to take a cut of their hard-earned money. Abolishing income tax—something that didn't even exist until 1913—could be the key to truly leveling the playing field and stripping politicians of their ability to weaponize taxation. In fact, it might solve many of the country's biggest problems—if Congress can stop tripping over itself.

My number one push button issue is and always will be taxes. That is, until we don't have to pay them anymore. We pay taxes at every turn in life, whether it's at the gas pump, property taxes, or in hidden tariffs built into the price of goods. But if we are going to reform the tax code, we need to understand it first. This book will offer a brief overview of the history of taxes in the United States, but will focus primarily on the Federal income tax. Federal income tax was not in the founders' plan, and it took an amendment to the Constitution to enable the government to levy such theft on its citizens. In my opinion, this single fix can level the playing field for all Americans and fix almost 90 percent of the nation's issues.

Taxes have played a fundamental role in shaping the relationship between the U.S. government and its citizens since the nation's founding. From early resistance to British taxation, taxes have remained central to how Americans view government authority, responsibility, and fairness. Over the centuries, the United States has shifted from relying primarily on tariffs and excise taxes to an income-based tax system. However, while the need for taxes is undisputed, the current U.S. tax system has become increasingly complex, inefficient, and unfair.

Today, our tax code spans tens of thousands of pages, filled with countless deductions, exemptions, and loopholes that favor the wealthy and burden the average taxpayer. The system places a disproportionate strain on middle and lower-income Americans, while those with the means to navigate the system can avoid paying their "fair share." As our country grows, so does dissatisfaction with a tax structure that no longer reflects the values of simplicity and fairness.

However, it's also fair to note that the highest earners in this country pay the most in Federal income taxes.

- The top 1% of earners (those with an income above approximately $580,000) pay around **40% of all federal income taxes.**
- The top 5% (incomes above approximately $250,000) pay about **60% of total federal income taxes.**
- The top 10% (incomes above roughly $150,000) contribute close to **70% of federal income taxes.**

This is a system that, while unduly straining lower-income Americans, also heavily taxes those who work hard and are most likely the job creators in this country. It's a system setup to discourage entrepreneurship and growth.

The answer to this problem is to fundamentally change how taxes are levied in the United States. In this book, I argue that abolishing income tax and replacing it with a Value-Added Tax (VAT) system, or a combination of tariffs and VAT, is the best way to simplify the tax system, promote fairness, and spur economic growth. You may have already heard VAT described as a 'fair' tax. VAT is fundamentally different from a flat tax or the progressive tax system we have today. A consumption-based tax like VAT would tax individuals and businesses on what they spend, not what they earn, leading to a more transparent and equitable system. A VAT system is also known as a fair tax because, as the name implies, everybody pays the same rate on what they spend. This is very different from a flat tax, where every taxpayer pays the same percentage rate on income. I firmly believe we need some form of taxes to fund the country, it's the income tax that I have a problem with.

When I talk to young people about the tax system in the United States, I frequently advocate for the abolition of the entirety of the tax code and moving to something fairer. I'm often met with statements like, "It's just part of life, it's the way it's always been!" They say things like, "You can't just take everything we've known and change it in one fell swoop!" Well, the truth is, the system hasn't always been like this. In fact, income tax is a little more than just 100 years old in our equally short history. The 16th amendment was the catalyst that made it possible for American citizens to have their income taxed. Before 1913, this was unconstitutional. It's necessary to briefly explore the history of taxation in the United States before I can explain how one simple change can fundamentally change the dynamic of our country for the better!

Early History of Taxation in the U.S.

The history of taxation in the United States begins long before the country achieved independence. During the colonial era, British taxes on the colonies sparked resistance and eventually rebellion. Taxes such as the Stamp Act of 1765 and the Townshend Acts of 1767 were imposed on the colonies without their consent, leading to the cry of "No taxation without representation." The discontent surrounding these taxes was one of the primary causes of the American Revolution, and the new nation's founders were cautious about how to structure taxation in the post-independence government. To put these early grievances in context, the taxation rate that the colonists were upset with was often less than 2%. Now, in certain areas of the country, the income tax rate can be well over 50 percent of one's earnings. Imagine having to give over half of what you earn to the government! A lot of you don't have to imagine.

After independence, the federal government initially relied on tariffs and excise taxes to fund its operations. The Tariff Act of 1789, the first major tax legislation passed by the U.S. government, imposed taxes on imported goods to protect domestic industries and generate revenue. Excise taxes, such as the tax on whiskey, were also used to raise funds. However, excise taxes were not without controversy. The Whiskey Rebellion of 1794, which saw farmers in western Pennsylvania revolt against the whiskey tax, highlighted the tension between federal authorities and taxpayers.

Throughout the 19th century, the federal government continued to rely on tariffs as its primary source of revenue. However, during the Civil War (1861–1865), the need for additional funds led Congress to introduce the first federal income tax in 1861. This tax was temporary, set at 3% on incomes over $800, but it established an important precedent. Although the income tax was repealed after the war, the idea of taxing income remained. It seemed crazy that this notion would ever become reality, yet here we are today, with most people working for months before they get to keep a dime of their own money.

This is often referred to as Tax Freedom Day. It's the day when the average taxpayer has theoretically earned enough income to pay off their total tax obligations for the year, including federal, state, and local taxes. The date usually falls somewhere in April but varies as some states may have a higher tax burden. I couldn't imagine explaining this to the colonists in the 1700s. I think their response to this proposal would be a hard NO!

By the late 19th century, as wealth concentrated in the hands of industrialists and corporate giants, there were growing calls for a permanent federal income tax to address rising inequality and provide the government with a reliable source of revenue. The limitations of relying solely on tariffs became increasingly apparent as the U.S. economy expanded and diversified. However, the introduction of a permanent income tax faced legal hurdles.

In 1894, Congress passed the Wilson-Gorman Tariff Act, which included a provision for a federal income tax, but the Supreme Court struck down the tax in Pollock v. Farmers' Loan & Trust Co. in 1895, ruling it unconstitutional. The court's decision declared that income taxes were "direct taxes" that needed to be apportioned among the states based on population, effectively blocking the government's ability to tax income at the federal level.

The 16th Amendment and Modern Income Tax

The constitutional barrier to a federal income tax was overcome in 1913 with the ratification of the 16th Amendment, which gave Congress the authority to levy taxes on income without apportioning them among the states. This marked a significant turning point in American tax policy. The idea of a new Federal tax on someone's income was initially met with limited resistance because it affected only a small proportion of the population. The tax rate started at just 1% on incomes above $3,000 (about $90,000 in today's dollars), with a top rate of 7% on incomes above $500,000 (over $15 million today). As a result, most Americans were not directly impacted, which softened widespread opposition.

This may explain why the 16th Amendment was passed at this time. It's important to note that to pass a constitutional amendment requires three of every four states to approve it, 38 out of 50. This process can begin either through a two-thirds vote in both houses of Congress or by a Constitutional convention called by two-thirds of state legislatures (34 states). Once proposed, the amendment must then be ratified by three-fourths of the states to become part of the Constitution. The process is riddled with hurdles for a multitude of reasons, but the parties making those decisions at the time may not have had enough foresight to see the full impact of their decisions, especially based on the metrics at the time.

Initially, the income tax applied only to the wealthiest Americans, but over the next few decades, the tax system expanded to cover a much larger proportion of the population. You may wonder if we would be having this conversation if today's percentages were still what they were in 1913. The answer is a definitive YES! Income taxes and redistribution of wealth is technically theft.

I want to give this argument a little perspective. In **1912**, before the introduction of an income tax, the U.S. federal debt was approximately **$1.15 billion**. In 2025, this figure would be approximately **$32.46 billion**, assuming an average annual inflation rate of around 3%. This was a period of relatively low federal borrowing, as the government operated under a philosophy of limited spending and largely balanced budgets.

The debt level at the time reflected pre-World War I policies and an economy that relied heavily on tariffs and excise taxes for revenue.

So with a federal debt of approximately **$1.15 billion** in 1912, and an estimated Gross Domestic Product (GDP) of around **$37 billion**, we can calculate the debt-to-GDP ratio: **3.1%.** This **debt-to-GDP ratio** highlights how minimal the federal debt was compared to the size of the economy. As of the second quarter of 2024, the United States' federal debt-to-GDP ratio was approximately **121.57%.** This indicates that the national debt exceeds the total annual economic output of the country.

Historically, the U.S. debt-to-GDP ratio has fluctuated, notably increasing during periods of economic downturns and significant government spending. For instance, the ratio rose sharply during the COVID-19 pandemic due to substantial fiscal stimulus measures. In 2020, it reached 126.24%, up from 100.12% in 2019. The current high debt-to-GDP ratio has raised concerns among economists and policymakers about the sustainability of federal borrowing and its potential impact on future economic growth. Addressing this issue may require a combination of fiscal policy adjustments, including spending cuts and revenue enhancements, to ensure long-term economic stability.

During World War I, the Great Depression, and World War II, the federal government significantly increased income tax rates to fund the war efforts and respond to economic crises. By the mid-20th century, the federal income tax had become the primary source of government revenue, applying to most working Americans and businesses. However, as the income tax system grew, so did its complexity. Over time, Congress introduced numerous deductions, credits, and exemptions aimed at promoting certain behaviors, such as homeownership or charitable giving. While these provisions benefited some, they also created a labyrinth of rules that became increasingly difficult to navigate. The tax code ballooned into an unwieldy system, where the wealthy could hire tax lawyers and accountants to find loopholes, while ordinary Americans were left to struggle with the complexities of filing their taxes.

The result has been a system where the wealthiest individuals and large corporations can significantly reduce their tax liabilities, often paying lower effective tax rates than middle-class wage earners. This has led to growing frustration with the fairness of the tax system and increasing calls for reform.

Problems with the Current Tax Code

The modern U.S. tax code is riddled with problems that undermine both its efficiency and fairness. At over 70,000 pages, the tax code is so complex that even professional accountants struggle to understand all its provisions. This complexity disproportionately affects middle-class and lower-income taxpayers, who often lack the resources to navigate the system or take advantage of its many deductions and credits. On a side note, one of the arguments I often hear in opposition to abolishing the tax code is that accountants would lose a lot of work... Really? It's the same argument I hear in NJ about passing a law that allows us to pump our own gas. You heard that correctly, we CANNOT pump our own gas in the state of New Jersey. In fact, we are the only state in the union with such a law. When someone wants to fix this so we can get on our way a little quicker without having to sit quietly and wait for an attendant, the argument is made that we can suffer the inconvenience because too many gas attendant jobs would be lost... Logical, right?

While the income tax system is theoretically progressive, meaning higher earners should pay a larger percentage of their income in taxes, in practice, many wealthy individuals use legal strategies to minimize their tax liabilities. Deductions, tax shelters, offshore accounts, and capital gains tax rates that are lower than income tax rates all contribute to the disparity between what high earners pay and what the average American pays.

Corporate taxation faces similar issues. Large multinational corporations, particularly in the tech and pharmaceutical industries, have become adept at shifting profits to low-tax jurisdictions to avoid paying U.S. taxes. Despite the official corporate tax rate being 21% after the 2017 Tax Cuts and Jobs Act, many large companies pay little to no federal income tax, creating an uneven playing field for small businesses that cannot take advantage of the same tax-avoidance strategies. And it's the smaller corporations that suffer. I own a few companies, and some are classified as an S Corporation. It is important to note that roughly 70% of the jobs created in America are created by small businesses like mine. The government is effectively penalizing most of the job creators, while the large corporations have more access to tax loopholes.

Another significant issue is tax evasion and avoidance. According to IRS estimates, the "tax gap"—the difference between taxes owed and taxes actually paid—totals hundreds of billions of dollars annually. Tax evasion is especially prevalent among high-income individuals and businesses that can exploit the complexity of the tax code to underreport income or overstate deductions. This widespread evasion undermines public trust in the tax system. Then again, the government created this monstrosity of a system, so they are essentially a victim of their own stupidity.

Finally, the tax code creates economic inefficiencies by distorting individual and business behavior. High marginal tax rates on income, capital gains, and dividends can discourage investment and savings, which are key drivers of economic growth. Many individuals and businesses make financial decisions based on minimizing taxes rather than maximizing productivity or innovation. This misallocation of resources hampers long-term economic growth and leaves the U.S. economy less competitive on the global stage.

Proposal: Abolish the Current Tax Code and Return to Tariffs or Implement a Value-Added Tax (VAT)

The undeniable problems with the current tax code make it clear that a fundamental overhaul is needed. Before the federal income tax was implemented in 1913, the U.S. government primarily funded itself through tariffs, excise taxes, and land sales. For much of the 19th century, these sources of revenue kept the budget balanced, and at times, the U.S. even ran surpluses. In the early 1800s, the national debt rose significantly due to the War of 1812, but President Andrew Jackson famously paid off the national debt entirely in 1835, the only time in U.S. history when the country had zero debt. However, debt levels rose again due to the Civil War (1861–1865), reaching around $2.7 billion by 1865. By the early 20th century, right before the income tax was enacted, the national debt was relatively low, around $2.9 billion, and there was generally no major budget deficit.

This begs the question: Could the U.S. feasibly raise enough revenue through tariffs to effectively run the country in its current circumstances? If we dig a little deeper for some more information, we can answer this question. We often fail to discuss the precise number the U.S. needs to "effectively" operate. While there may be varying opinions on this, it's abundantly clear that there is a lot of waste, fraud, and abuse in the Federal budget. When we decide to trim the fat, we may find that the number needed to operate effectively is much lower than previously thought. However, if tariffs aren't a magic wand, there is a fairer approach that affects all Americans equally and proportionately, it's called a VAT!

A Value-Added Tax (VAT) is a compelling alternative to the existing income-based tax system. VAT is a consumption tax applied to goods and services at each stage of production and distribution. However, if a VAT tax were to be implemented here in the United States, it would work like a state sales tax does. Only the end users pay the sales taxes. If someone is buying goods or services for resale, those portions of purchases are tax-exempt. We can and should only implement a VAT system the same way states impose a sales tax to protect against overwhelming inflation. Unlike income taxes, which tax individuals based on their earnings, VAT taxes individuals based on what they consume.

VAT is widely used across the world, particularly in Europe, Canada, and Japan, where it has proven to be a reliable and efficient means of raising revenue. By shifting from an income-based tax to a consumption-based tax, the U.S. can create a simpler, fairer, and more stable tax system that encourages saving and investment while reducing opportunities for tax evasion and avoidance.

One of the primary advantages of VAT is its simplicity. Individuals no longer need to file annual income tax returns, and businesses collect VAT at the point of sale, making the tax process more straightforward and transparent. This eliminates much of the administrative burden that currently falls on taxpayers and reduces opportunities for tax fraud. This also allows for a complete overhaul of the Internal Revenue Service. The IRS could be streamlined to a fraction of the size it currently is and would save taxpayers additional money.

VAT also promotes fairness by ensuring that everyone pays taxes based on what they consume. Wealthier individuals, who tend to spend more on luxury goods and services, will naturally pay more in taxes, while low-income individuals can be protected through exemptions for basic necessities like food, healthcare, and housing. Additionally, VAT is harder to evade than income tax because it is collected at the point of sale, along with any state and local sales taxes.

Furthermore, VAT encourages economic growth by taxing consumption rather than income. Under the current system, individuals and businesses are penalized for earning more, which can discourage entrepreneurship and investment. In contrast, VAT allows people to save and invest without being penalized for their success. This shift in incentives can promote long-term economic growth, as individuals and businesses have more freedom to reinvest their earnings and expand operations. With a VAT system, economic decisions are more likely to be driven by market forces and productivity rather than by tax considerations, leading to a more efficient allocation of resources.

One of the main drivers of proposing a VAT system is the fact that roughly 40% of American citizens don't pay a single dime in income tax. However, these same citizens have equal voting rights, giving them a say in wealth distribution. The system is entirely unfair. Abolishing income tax and scrapping the entirety of the tax code would truly level the playing field. This would ensure that everyone in the country has some skin in the game. It would also spur a conversation on a much larger measure: spending. The 40% of Americans who don't pay anything in income taxes surely shouldn't have a say in where the country is spending its revenue, after all, it's not their money. However, if they were contributing, the consequences would affect them equally. This may cause a more relevant conversation on why taxes are so high and why the government is spending so much.

Another significant advantage of VAT is the stability it provides in government revenue. Because VAT is based on consumption, it tends to be more stable than income tax, which fluctuates with the economy. During economic downturns, income tax revenues often fall sharply as people lose jobs or see their incomes reduced. In contrast, consumption remains relatively steady, even in times of economic difficulty, as people continue to buy essential goods and services. This makes VAT a more predictable source of revenue, helping the government maintain funding for vital services, even during recessions.

Implementation and Transition Challenges to VAT

Implementing a Value-Added Tax in the United States would represent a significant shift in how the government collects revenue, and such a transition must be carefully planned to ensure success. One of the primary challenges would be phasing out the current income tax system while introducing VAT gradually. Abruptly eliminating income tax could lead to revenue shortfalls and economic disruption, so a phased approach would be necessary.

The transition plan could begin by introducing VAT at a low rate—such as 5% to 10%—while gradually reducing income tax rates over several years. This would give businesses and consumers time to adjust to the new tax structure without causing economic shock. As VAT becomes a more significant source of revenue, the income tax could eventually be eliminated altogether. However, a transition could give the government an opportunity to keep both tax bases like a system that Canada currently has. To make this work fairly, income tax needs to become unconstitutional again.

Protecting low-income households during a transition is also critical. One of the most common criticisms of VAT is that it can be regressive, meaning it disproportionately affects lower-income individuals who spend a larger percentage of their income on consumption. To address this concern, essential goods such as food, healthcare, and education should be exempt from VAT, as is done in many countries that have implemented the tax. Additionally, targeted rebates or credits could be provided to low-income individuals and families to offset the VAT they pay on necessities.

Another important consideration is the impact of VAT on small businesses. Small businesses often face higher administrative burdens when complying with tax laws, and VAT could increase these costs if not implemented carefully. To mitigate this, the government could introduce simplified VAT filing procedures for small businesses or set a threshold below which businesses are exempt from VAT registration. This would reduce the burden on very small businesses and ensure that the system is not overly complex for those who lack the resources to manage detailed tax filings.

Coordination between federal, state, and local governments is also essential. Many states already have sales taxes, and implementing a federal VAT could create confusion or duplication if not carefully managed. The federal government could work with state governments to harmonize VAT with existing sales taxes or even replace state sales taxes with a portion of the VAT revenue. This would create a more streamlined system, reducing the administrative burden on businesses and ensuring that consumers are not faced with multiple layers of taxation.

Public perception and political support are perhaps the most significant challenges in implementing VAT. Many Americans are unfamiliar with VAT, and there is likely to be resistance to what may be perceived as a new tax. To address this, the government must engage in a comprehensive public education campaign that explains the benefits of VAT, particularly its ability to simplify the tax system, promote fairness, and stabilize government revenue.

Finally, gaining bipartisan political support for VAT would require building a broad coalition of stakeholders. Republicans may favor VAT for its potential to encourage economic growth and reduce the size of government by eliminating income taxes, while Democrats may appreciate its ability to generate stable revenue and reduce income inequality through targeted rebates and exemptions. Ensuring that the VAT system is designed to be fair and transparent will be key to securing the necessary political buy-in.

The Benefits of Transitioning to VAT

The benefits of transitioning to a Value-Added Tax system are far-reaching, impacting individuals, businesses, and the broader U.S. economy. The first and most immediate benefit is the simplification of the tax system. The complexity of the current U.S. tax code is a significant burden on both taxpayers and the government. Individuals spend hours each year filing complicated tax returns, and businesses often require professional assistance to comply with the myriad rules and regulations, sorry accountants! VAT eliminates much of this complexity, making the tax system more transparent and easier to navigate. With VAT, individuals no longer need to file annual tax returns, and businesses face a simpler process for collecting and remitting taxes.

VAT also promotes fairness by ensuring that taxes are based on consumption rather than income. This means that those who spend more—often wealthier individuals—will pay more in taxes, while those who spend less, particularly lower-income households, can be protected through exemptions and rebates. This system is inherently more equitable than the current income tax structure, which allows the wealthiest Americans to minimize their tax burden through deductions, loopholes, and tax shelters.

Furthermore, VAT encourages economic growth by taxing consumption rather than income. Under the current system, individuals and businesses are penalized for earning more money, which can discourage investment, savings, and entrepreneurship. VAT, on the other hand, incentivizes saving and investment by taxing individuals only when they choose to spend. This shift can lead to higher levels of capital formation and long-term economic growth, as businesses have more freedom to reinvest their profits and expand operations.

Another critical benefit of VAT is the stability it provides in government revenue. Because VAT is based on consumption, it is less affected by economic fluctuations than income tax. During economic downturns, when incomes fall and people lose jobs, income tax revenues typically decline, creating budgetary challenges for the government. In contrast, consumption tends to remain relatively stable, even during recessions, ensuring that the government has a steady stream of revenue to fund essential services.

Finally, VAT can make the U.S. economy more competitive in the global marketplace. By reducing the tax burden on income and profits, VAT allows businesses to focus on growth and innovation rather than tax planning. This can make the U.S. a more attractive destination for foreign investment and help domestic

companies compete more effectively against international com-
petitors. Many of the world's leading economies have already
adopted VAT, and transitioning to a similar system would bring
the U.S. tax structure more in line with global norms. However,
some even argue against a VAT system and income taxes all
together, proposing to fund our government with tariffs alone.

Tariffs Only

In the early years of U.S. history, tariffs were indeed the primary
source of federal government revenue. For much of the 19th
century and into the early 20th century, tariffs on imported
goods funded a significant portion of government operations.
However, the ability of the U.S. to fully fund its government
on tariffs alone today is highly unlikely due to several factors:

1. Federal Government Size and Scope

- In the early 20th century, the federal government was much
  smaller, with limited responsibilities compared to today.
- Federal spending in 1913 was less than **2% of GDP**,
  while in recent years, federal spending has been around
  20-25% of GDP. This is why DOGE has become essential. With the government failing to impose spending
  constraints, an external influence was needed to finally
  rein in expenditures.
- Modern responsibilities, such as Social Security,
  Medicare, defense, education, and infrastructure, require far greater revenue than tariffs could generate.

2. Modern Trade Dynamics

- The U.S. economy is much more integrated with global
  trade today. Imposing high tariffs could discourage im-
  ports, reducing the potential revenue.

- In 2022, U.S. tariff revenue was approximately **$100 billion**, while federal expenditures were over **$6 trillion**—tariffs cover only about **1.7%** of spending.

3. Economic Impacts of High Tariffs

- High tariffs could lead to retaliatory measures by trading partners, hurting exports and economic growth.
- They could increase the cost of imported goods for consumers and businesses, leading to inflationary pressures.

4. Revenue Composition

- Today, federal revenues primarily come from **income taxes** (individual and corporate) and **payroll taxes**, which are far more significant sources of funding than tariffs.

While tariffs were sufficient to fund the government in the 19th century due to its smaller size and simpler role, the modern federal government relies on a broader tax base. Funding today's government solely on tariffs is not feasible without dramatically reducing the scope of federal activities or imposing high tariffs, which would have significant economic consequences depending on how they are implemented and on whom. The conversation again is centered on spending. I am hoping the Department of Government Efficiency (DOGE) can do its job and make our government so small that we don't have to have these conversations anymore. Shrinking the size of government so that we live within our means would mean restoring many of the freedoms we have lost over the last century, giving power and control back to the American people.

Conclusion

The U.S. tax system is long overdue for reform. The complexity, inefficiency, and inequity of the current income tax code have made it unsustainable in the face of modern economic challenges. By replacing income tax with a Value-Added Tax, or a combination of both VAT and tariffs, the United States can build a fairer, simpler, and more stable tax system that encourages economic growth and ensures that everyone contributes equally and fairly. More importantly, VAT doesn't pick winners and losers in the system. This is the only way to fundamentally stop the inherent segregation that the current tax code is responsible for.

VAT is not a new or untested idea. It has been successfully implemented in many countries around the world, providing a stable and reliable source of revenue while promoting fairness and reducing opportunities for tax evasion. With the right design and implementation strategy, VAT can help the United States address its fiscal challenges, promote economic growth, and build a tax system that works for all Americans.

While this book will offer many solutions to save America, the tax code is most likely the most important of them all. The complexities of the current tax code are not just a burden on the economy—they are a burden on the American people. Scrapping the current tax code offers a path forward—a path that ensures America remains competitive in the global economy while providing the resources needed to build a better future for all its citizens, fairly!

3

TERM LIMITS

THE CONCEPT OF TERM LIMITS FOR elected officials has long been debated in the United States. While the presidency has been limited to two terms since the passage of the 22nd Amendment in 1951, members of Congress remain free to serve unlimited terms, as long as they continue to win re-election. This has led to concerns about career politicians, the entrenchment of power, and the erosion of accountability. Despite the popularity of the idea among voters, efforts to impose term limits on Congress have repeatedly failed to gain traction.

In this chapter, I will explore the history of term limits in the United States, both at the federal and state levels, as well as examine how other countries have addressed the issue. I will argue that term limits are a necessary reform to restore accountability and promote fresh ideas in government.

The History of Term Limits in the U.S.

Term limits have been a topic of discussion since the early days of the United States. The Founding Fathers had mixed views on the idea, with some, like Thomas Jefferson, expressing support for limiting how long an individual could hold office. However, the U.S. Constitution, as drafted, did not include term limits for any federal offices, allowing members of Congress to serve indefinitely if they were re-elected.

The Founding Fathers of the United States generally expressed skepticism about the idea of career politicians, emphasizing that public service should be a temporary role, not a lifelong pursuit. They believed that political power should not be concentrated in the hands of a few individuals over long periods of time, as it could lead to corruption and tyranny, which is what seems to have happened as of late. Here are some relevant perspectives from key founders:

1. George Washington

Washington set a strong precedent by voluntarily stepping down after two terms as president, even though he could have stayed longer. In his Farewell Address (1796), he warned against the dangers of the "love of power" and the concentration of power in the hands of a few. He believed in returning to private life after public service. This voluntary precedent was quietly abided by until Franklin D. Roosevelt during the Second World War. Washington was quoted saying, "The spirit of encroachment tends to consolidate the powers of all the departments in one, and thus to create whatever the form of government, a real despotism."

2. Thomas Jefferson

Jefferson was critical of entrenched political elites. He believed that the government should be renewed by regular turnover of its leaders and was an advocate for term limits. He was concerned that those who stay in power for too long would grow detached from the people and become corrupt. On these issues, Jefferson said, "Whenever a man has cast a longing eye on offices, a rottenness begins in his conduct." He also argued for the rotation of office, believing that frequent elections were necessary to keep government accountable to the people.

3. James Madison

Madison shared similar concerns about the dangers of concentrated power. In Federalist No. 57, he argued that frequent elections would serve as a check on career politicians, ensuring that representatives would stay accountable to their constituents. He once said, "The aim of every political constitution is, or ought to be, first to obtain for rulers' men who possess most wisdom to discern, and most virtue to pursue, the common good of the society; and in the next place, to take the most effectual precautions for keeping them virtuous whilst they continue to hold their public trust."

4. Benjamin Franklin

Franklin also expressed the view that public service should not be a career but a civic duty, and those who remain in office too long may grow selfish. His voice resonates with my position on this issue the most, saying, "In free governments, the rulers are the servants, and the people their superiors and sovereigns. For the former to return among the latter does not degrade but promote them." Here he is emphasizing how it's more honorable to serve and return to private life.

5. John Adams

Adams was concerned about the potential for a hereditary aristocracy or political elite to form. He supported the idea of a rotation in office to prevent any one person or group from becoming too powerful. He stated, "There is danger from all men. The only maxim of a free government ought to be to trust no man living with power to endanger the public liberty."

6. Thomas Paine

Although not a member of the Constitutional Convention, Paine's writings, like *Common Sense*, greatly influenced the Revolutionary spirit. He was a staunch advocate of limited government and believed that career politicians would lose touch with the common people and prioritize their own interests. He once said, "That there should be no offices of profit, nor the people be burdened with the maintenance of useless officers, and that politicians should not be suffered to continue in office long enough to accumulate wealth or power."

While the Founders did not explicitly use the modern term "career politicians," they expressed concerns about the dangers of political entrenchment and the concentration of power. They envisioned public service as a temporary duty rather than a lifelong career and advocated for regular turnover to maintain a government that is responsive and accountable to the people. Many of their views laid the groundwork for ideas like term limits and the need for checks and balances in government. I believe that if the founders could see what the future held for our country and how the system currently works, they would have incorporated some form of term limitations for Congress.

The first notable change in this area came after President Franklin D. Roosevelt broke with tradition by serving four terms as president during the Great Depression and World War II. His extended tenure sparked concerns about the dangers of executive overreach and the potential for the presidency to become a de facto monarchy. In response, Congress passed the 22nd Amendment in 1947, which was ratified by the states in 1951, limiting presidents to two terms.

While presidential term limits were widely accepted, the idea of imposing similar limits on Congress has faced significant resistance. Throughout the 20th and 21st centuries, numerous attempts have been made to introduce term limits for senators and representatives, but these efforts have consistently failed. The most notable push came during the Republican-led "Contract with America" initiative in the 1990s, when the Republican Party, led by Newt Gingrich, proposed a constitutional amendment to impose term limits on Congress in the House of Representatives on March 29, 1995. The proposal aimed to amend the Constitution to limit members of Congress to a set number of terms—specifically, six two-year terms for House members (12 years) and two six-year terms for senators (12 years).

The House voted on four separate term-limit proposals, with the most supported proposal receiving a majority of 227-204 but failing to meet the two-thirds supermajority required for a constitutional amendment. The Senate also attempted to pass term limits around this time but similarly failed to achieve the necessary support. A constitutional amendment proposal needs a two-thirds majority in both chambers and ratification by three-fourths of the states, which remains a high bar that term-limit proposals have not met.

At the state level, however, term limits have gained more traction. Many states have implemented term limits for governors, state legislators, and other elected officials. Currently, 15 states impose term limits on their legislatures, with varying restrictions on how many consecutive terms members can serve. Those states include **Arizona, Arkansas, California, Colorado, Florida, Louisiana, Maine, Michigan, Missouri, Montana, Nebraska (unicameral legislature), Nevada, Ohio, Oklahoma, and South Dakota**. These term limits vary in length and apply differently depending on the state. Most commonly, they limit legislators to serving a maximum number of consecutive terms in one chamber, but some allow legislators to serve additional terms after a break.

According to a 2022 Gallup poll, about 82% of U.S. adults are in favor of implementing term limits for members of Congress. This support crosses party lines, with **89% of Republicans**, **83% of independents**, and **74% of Democrats** expressing their approval of term limits. As the support for term limits has grown in recent years, it has become more apparent that the public's frustration with Congress is at a tipping point.

Term Limits in Other Countries

While the U.S. has been slow to adopt term limits for its legislative branch, many other countries have embraced them as a way to ensure turnover in government and limit the potential for corruption. Below are a few notable examples of how term limits have been implemented around the world:

- **Mexico:** In Mexico, term limits are strictly enforced at all levels of government. The president is limited to a single six-year term with no possibility of re-election. Members of both houses of Congress are also subject to term limits: senators can serve up to two consecutive six-year terms, and deputies in the lower house can serve up to four three-year terms. These restrictions were implemented to prevent the rise of powerful, long-serving politicians and ensure regular turnover in the government.

- **France:** France imposes a limit on its presidency, with presidents allowed to serve a maximum of two consecutive five-year terms. However, no term limits exist for members of the French National Assembly or Senate, meaning legislators can remain in office indefinitely, similar to the current system in the United States.

- ⊚ **South Korea:** In South Korea, the president is limited to a single five-year term, with no possibility of re-election. This restriction was established in response to the authoritarian rule of previous leaders and is seen as a safeguard against potential abuses of power.
- ⊚ **Brazil:** In Brazil, the president is limited to two consecutive four-year terms. However, unlike the U.S., Brazilian presidents are allowed to run for office again after sitting out a term. This system allows for the possibility of a leader returning to power while still maintaining a safeguard against excessive entrenchment.

Term limits in these countries have been implemented to prevent political dynasties, reduce corruption, and foster a dynamic political environment. These examples demonstrate that term limits can work in diverse political systems and that limiting the tenure of elected officials can promote accountability and encourage new leadership.

Why the U.S. Desperately Needs Term Limits

In the U.S., the absence of term limits for Congress has allowed politicians to remain in office for decades, often resulting in stagnation, partisanship, and a disconnection from the concerns of ordinary Americans. The longer a politician remains in office, the more entrenched they become in the political establishment, leading to a system where incumbents are overwhelmingly re-elected and new voices are marginalized.

One of the most significant consequences of the lack of term limits is the rise of career politicians—individuals who spend the majority of their professional lives in Congress. While experience in government can be valuable, it also carries the risk of insulating politicians from the realities faced by their constituents. Long-serving members of Congress often become more focused on maintaining their power and securing re-election than on addressing the pressing issues of the day. This dynamic can lead to a disconnect between the public and their elected representatives, as well as the prioritization of special interests over the needs of the electorate.

As I've stated on my show many times, you may have the best intentions when you first run for Congress, but with a short 2-year term, it's almost impossible not to become immediately entrenched in the system. Members of Congress essentially never stop running for office. The moment they are elected they are right back out on the campaign trail. In addition, if a fiscal conservative runs for office, the likelihood of getting re-elected becomes slimmer if they can't bring dollars back to their district. That requires compromise and spending that might not necessarily be good for the country but may allow them to keep their job if the district is flourishing. Let's face it, politicians are never going to get a bridge or a school named after them unless they are bringing home the bacon!

Term limits would help solve this problem by ensuring regular turnover in Congress. New members would bring fresh perspectives and ideas, while also being less beholden to the entrenched interests that dominate Washington. By limiting how long members of Congress can serve, we can reduce the influence of lobbyists, political donors, and other actors who benefit from the status quo. Moreover, term limits would encourage lawmakers to focus on long-term solutions rather than short-term political calculations aimed at securing their next election.

Another key benefit of term limits is they would restore accountability to the legislative process. Today, incumbents (those already holding office and running for re-election) enjoy significant advantages in fundraising, name recognition, and media coverage, making it difficult for challengers to unseat them. As a result, Congress has an extraordinarily high re-election rate, even when public approval of the institution is at historic lows. By implementing term limits, we can level the playing field, giving voters more opportunities to elect new representatives who are truly accountable to the public.

Finally, term limits would help address the partisanship and gridlock that have plagued Congress in recent years. When politicians know they can remain in office indefinitely, they may be more likely to dig in their heels and refuse to compromise, knowing they have little risk of being replaced. Term limits would create a sense of urgency, encouraging lawmakers to work together to achieve meaningful results during their limited time in office.

Overcoming Political Resistance: Grandfathering Current Members

One of the primary obstacles to implementing term limits is the political reality that members of Congress are unlikely to vote for a measure that would limit their own careers. Self-preservation is a powerful motivator, and many lawmakers who have spent decades in office are unlikely to support a system that would force them to leave. They will argue that term limits already exist in the case where the citizens can just vote them out in the next cycle. You and I both know that once someone is in office, it becomes very hard to get them out.

To overcome this challenge, Congress could implement term limits with a "grandfather clause" that exempts current members from the new restrictions. This would allow sitting members of Congress to serve out their careers without being affected by the term limits they impose on future generations of lawmakers. While this might seem like a compromise, it could make the idea of term limits more politically palatable, as members would not have to vote against their own interests.

Grandfathering current members would provide a way to introduce term limits without upending the careers of those already in the office. More importantly, it would ensure that future members of Congress are subject to the new rules, preventing the rise of entrenched political dynasties and promoting a healthier, more dynamic legislative environment.

The re-election rate of incumbents in the United States is very high, especially at the federal level. Incumbents tend to have significant advantages over challengers, such as name recognition, established donor networks, and greater media visibility. Here are the general statistics based on recent years:

Congress (U.S. House of Representatives and Senate):

1. **U.S. House of Representatives:**
    - The re-election rate for incumbents in the House has typically been around **90-95%**. In some election cycles, it can be slightly lower or higher depending on political factors such as national sentiment or significant political movements, but the general trend shows high retention rates.

2. **U.S. Senate:**

- The Senate re-election rate is slightly lower than the House but still quite high, generally around **80-90%**. Senate races tend to be more competitive since Senators serve six-year terms, and there are fewer seats, but incumbents still maintain a strong advantage.

Reasons for High Incumbency Re-election Rates:

- **Name Recognition:** Voters are more likely to support a familiar name on the ballot.
- **Campaign Fundraising:** Incumbents often have better access to campaign funds, making it easier for them to run successful campaigns.
- **Constituent Services:** Incumbents can point to specific services they've provided to their constituents, creating a stronger personal connection.
- **Gerrymandering:** In the House, district boundaries can be drawn to favor incumbents or their party, making re-election more likely.
- **Weak Challengers:** Incumbents often face weaker opponents, as the best challengers may wait for an open seat rather than contesting a popular incumbent.

Term limits are a vital reform that the United States needs to restore accountability, encourage new leadership, and reduce the influence of special interests in government. By looking at examples from other countries, it's clear that term limits can help prevent the entrenchment of power and promote political renewal and corruption.

In the U.S., implementing term limits for Congress would help break the cycle of career politicians and force lawmakers to focus on the people they represent rather than their political survival. While political resistance is inevitable, offering to "grandfather" in current members of Congress would make the transition smoother and ensure that future generations benefit from the new system. It's ironic that in a government of, by, and for the people, we must acquiesce to the fact that this is the last thing they care about. Maybe in 40 years, our children's children will finally see the last entrenched politician leave office.

It's time to bring fresh voices and new ideas to Washington. Term limits are not just a popular idea—they're a necessary step toward making government more responsive to the people and more effective at addressing the challenges of our time. It also ensures that we can begin tightening the reins on corruption and help save America from career politicians once and for all.

4

A BALANCED BUDGET AMENDMENT

WHILE THE ISSUES OUTLINED IN THE first few chapters of this book would, in my opinion, solve most of the problems in the United States, several often-overlooked issues could also play a major role in saving America. In this chapter, we look at our country's fiscal responsibility. Since Congress doesn't seem to know how to balance a checkbook, it may be time for a balanced budget amendment. The United States Congress is often called the keeper of the nation's purse, as they are constitutionally entrusted with controlling the treasury, but if members of Congress were bookkeepers in a business, they would have been fired long ago for their poor financial management. Over the years, Congress has demonstrated an alarming disregard for fiscal responsibility, repeatedly passing bloated budgets, running up trillions in debt, and funding unnecessary programs (such as those shockingly exposed by Elon Musk and his team at DOGE), while ignoring long-term economic consequences. This reckless approach has burdened the American taxpayer with an unsustainable financial legacy that jeopardizes the nation's economic stability.

The debate over fiscal responsibility in the United States government has been a persistent and often polarizing issue ever since the founding of the Republic. At the heart of this debate lies the question of whether the government should be required by law to balance its budget, meaning federal spending could not exceed federal revenue. The idea is simple, right?

I've heard someone say, "If I ran my household budget like this, I'd be homeless," or a business owner say, "If I spent the way the government spends, I would have been out of business a long time ago." This idea has gained prominence through repeated calls for a constitutional amendment—the Balanced Budget Amendment (BBA)—that would legally enforce fiscal discipline.

Again, balancing a budget is a very basic principle which is necessary for the financial health of a household or an entire nation. A household can't spend more than they take in, right? Well, it theoretically could, but the person who runs that household would have to borrow the money it didn't have in the form of credit. Simple enough, until the creditors come calling and the banks come to claim their collateral. But it doesn't quite work that way for the Federal government. The Feds can just print more money. The problem with this is it devalues the currency that is already in circulation by causing inflation, and inflation affects everyone equally! The story could go in a multitude of directions, but the bottom line is that our government can't seem to balance a budget on their own, so maybe it's time to force them to do so!

Proponents of a balanced budget amendment argue that such an amendment is necessary to curb reckless government spending, reduce the national debt, and ensure long-term economic stability. Opponents, however, contend that a BBA could impose rigid constraints on the government's ability to respond to economic crises and social needs. Personally, I think the government needs to spend within its means, and that means we need to babysit. While the first two issues outlined in this book solve a lot of these problems, we simply can't have a government that doesn't understand or even care about the economic health of the country. They callously pass spending bill after spending bill without concern for the generations that will succeed them. Those massive omnibus bills that some lawmakers passionately advocate for now appear dubious in light of new revelations emerging from DOGE.

Below, we will explore the history of proposed balanced budget amendments in the United States, tracing their origins, and examining the evolution of political discourse surrounding them and the opposition that has consistently thwarted their adoption. By delving into the political and ideological viewpoints on a balanced budget, this chapter will also present the case for why such an amendment is more necessary today than ever before.

Early Calls for Fiscal Discipline: The Founding Era

The Founding Fathers, while deeply concerned with fiscal prudence, did not include a balanced budget requirement in the U.S. Constitution. However, their writings and actions reflected a commitment to avoiding excessive debt and ensuring sound financial practices. Alexander Hamilton, the nation's first Secretary of the Treasury, was a proponent of a strong central government capable of managing national finances, but he also believed that debt must be used responsibly. He argued that debt could be a "national blessing" if kept within manageable limits and used to fund essential infrastructure, but he warned that unchecked borrowing could weaken the nation.

Thomas Jefferson, by contrast, was more wary of public debt and favored a more stringent approach to balancing the government's books. In 1798, Jefferson wrote to John Taylor of Caroline about his belief that the government should avoid debt altogether, stating, "I place economy among the first and most important republican virtues, and public debt as the greatest of the dangers to be feared." Jefferson's fear of debt stemmed from a belief that future generations should not be burdened by the financial obligations of their predecessors.

Though these early debates established the necessity of fiscal responsibility, no constitutional mechanisms were introduced to mandate a balanced budget. The federal government's borrowing powers were left open-ended in the Constitution, and no formal requirement for fiscal balance was considered during the drafting process. While the founders were well-intentioned, I ask myself, what if they could have seen into the future? Would the founders go back and amend their original document if they knew then what we know now? As a constitutional conservative, I don't like to play around with what is stated in the Constitution, but since this provision isn't included, I often wonder if this is something that was overlooked. One must look to the past to understand the founders' intentions, particularly regarding debt.

U.S. national debt has fluctuated under different presidents due to varying economic policies, wars, recessions, and other factors. Below is a summary of significant moments in America's history of national debt under various presidents, showing how it changed during their respective terms. The amounts are approximate, reflecting the debt at the start and end of each presidency, with the understanding that fiscal policies take time to show their full impact. The debt figures are sourced from the U.S. Treasury and other historical data.

1. George Washington (1789–1797)
- **National Debt at Start:** $75 million
- **National Debt at End:** $83 million
- **Change:** +$8 million

Under George Washington, the U.S. national debt was consolidated and assumed by the federal government after the Revolutionary War. Alexander Hamilton, as Treasury Secretary, established mechanisms to manage and repay the debt.

2. Thomas Jefferson (1801-1809)
- **National Debt at Start:** $83 million
- **National Debt at End:** $57 million
- **Change:** -$26 million

Jefferson focused on reducing the national debt through spending cuts, although the Louisiana Purchase in 1803 increased debt temporarily.

3. Andrew Jackson (1829-1837)
- **National Debt at Start:** $58 million
- **National Debt at End:** $33,000 (almost zero)
- **Change:** -$58 million

Jackson is the only president to have effectively paid off the national debt. He was vehemently opposed to national debt and fought to eliminate it.

4. Abraham Lincoln (1861-1865)
- **National Debt at Start:** $65 million
- **National Debt at End:** $2.7 billion
- **Change:** +$2.64 billion

The Civil War caused an unprecedented increase in the national debt due to the massive costs of the conflict.

5. Woodrow Wilson (1913–1921)

- ◉ **National Debt at Start:** $2.9 billion
- ◉ **National Debt at End:** $24 billion
- ◉ **Change:** +$21.1 billion

Wilson's administration saw the national debt rise significantly because of World War I and the subsequent post-war recovery efforts. Woodrow Wilson was also a very progressive president, and it was in his term that income tax became legal. In total, three constitutional amendments were passed during his presidency, and it marked the start of the more progressive amendments to the Constitution.

6. Franklin D. Roosevelt (1933–1945)

- ◉ **National Debt at Start:** $22 billion
- ◉ **National Debt at End:** $258 billion
- ◉ **Change:** +$236 billion

The Great Depression and World War II dramatically increased the national debt under FDR. The New Deal and war spending were major factors.

7. Harry S. Truman (1945–1953)

- ◉ **National Debt at Start:** $258 billion
- ◉ **National Debt at End:** $266 billion
- ◉ **Change:** +$8 billion

Truman inherited the debt from World War II and saw modest increases during his administration, largely due to the Korean War.

8. Dwight D. Eisenhower (1953–1961)
- ⊙ **National Debt at Start:** $266 billion
- ⊙ **National Debt at End:** $288 billion
- ⊙ **Change:** +$22 billion

Eisenhower increased military spending during the Cold War but was relatively fiscally conservative, leading to only modest increases in debt.

9. John F. Kennedy (1961–1963)
- ⊙ **National Debt at Start:** $288 billion
- ⊙ **National Debt at End:** $305 billion
- ⊙ **Change:** +$17 billion

Kennedy's brief time in office saw modest increases in the national debt, primarily due to defense spending and tax cuts.

10. Lyndon B. Johnson (1963–1969)
- ⊙ **National Debt at Start:** $305 billion
- ⊙ **National Debt at End:** $369 billion
- ⊙ **Change:** +$64 billion

Johnson's "Great Society" programs and the Vietnam War significantly contributed to the increase in the national debt during his tenure.

11. Richard Nixon (1969–1974)
- ⊙ **National Debt at Start:** $369 billion
- ⊙ **National Debt at End:** $475 billion
- ⊙ **Change:** +$106 billion

Nixon's administration saw increased spending on social programs, the Vietnam War, and inflation, which drove the debt higher.

12. Jimmy Carter (1977–1981)
- **National Debt at Start:** $699 billion
- **National Debt at End:** $900 billion
- **Change:** +$201 billion

Carter's administration faced stagflation, energy crises, and increased spending on social programs, which contributed to the rising debt. **Stagflation** is an economic condition characterized by the simultaneous occurrence of **high inflation, stagnant economic growth, and high unemployment**. It is considered an unusual and challenging situation because inflation and economic stagnation are typically seen as opposing forces.

13. Ronald Reagan (1981–1989)
- **National Debt at Start:** $900 billion
- **National Debt at End:** $2.7 trillion
- **Change:** +$1.8 trillion

Reagan's administration saw one of the largest increases in the national debt, driven by military spending during the Cold War and increases in entitlement spending. **Entitlement spending** refers to government expenditure on programs that provide benefits to individuals who meet certain eligibility requirements. These programs are typically **mandatory spending**, meaning they are funded automatically each year without requiring annual approval from Congress, i.e., **Social Security, Medicare and Medicaid**.

14. George H. W. Bush (1989–1993)
- ⊙ **National Debt at Start:** $2.7 trillion
- ⊙ **National Debt at End:** $4.2 trillion
- ⊙ **Change:** +$1.5 trillion

Bush faced rising deficits due to the Persian Gulf War, tax cuts, and continued entitlement spending. The recession of the early 1990s also increased deficits.

15. Bill Clinton (1993–2001)
- ⊙ **National Debt at Start:** $4.2 trillion
- ⊙ **National Debt at End:** $5.7 trillion
- ⊙ **Change:** +$1.5 trillion

Clinton's administration initially increased the national debt, but later in his presidency, budget surpluses were achieved from 1998 to 2001 due to economic growth, spending restraint, and tax increases, reducing the deficit.

16. George W. Bush (2001–2009)
- ⊙ **National Debt at Start:** $5.7 trillion
- ⊙ **National Debt at End:** $10.6 trillion
- ⊙ **Change:** +$4.9 trillion

The debt rose sharply under Bush due to the 2001 and 2003 tax cuts, the wars in Iraq and Afghanistan, and the financial crisis of 2008, which necessitated government bailouts and stimulus packages.

17. Barack Obama (2009–2017)
- **National Debt at Start:** $10.6 trillion
- **National Debt at End:** $19.9 trillion
- **Change:** +$9.3 trillion

Obama inherited the Great Recession, leading to large-scale stimulus spending and bailouts. The Affordable Care Act, continued military spending, and tax policies also contributed to the rising debt.

18. Donald Trump (2017–2021)
- **National Debt at Start:** $19.9 trillion
- **National Debt at End:** $27.8 trillion
- **Change:** +$7.9 trillion

The national debt increased significantly during Trump's administration due to increased defense spending and the federal government's response to the **COVID-19 pandemic** through relief measures such as the CARES Act.

19. Joe Biden (2021–2025)
- **National Debt at Start:** $27.8 trillion
- **National Debt as of March 2025:** Over $36 trillion
- **Change:** +$8.4 trillion

Biden's administration saw a further increase in the national debt, driven by continued spending to address the COVID-19 pandemic, infrastructure investments, and expanded social programs like the American Rescue Plan and Inflation Reduction Act.

The First Proposals for a BBA: The Progressive Era and the New Deal

The first serious proposals for a balanced budget amendment came in the early 20th century, during the Progressive Era and the economic upheavals of the 1920s and 1930s. Government spending had increased significantly leading up to and during this period, particularly during World War I. As a result, concerns about the federal government's fiscal practices began to mount. As a side note, I must comment on my usage of the word "progressive." Most people look at the root of the word and assume that "progressive" must involve our interpretation of the word "progress." This is simply not the case when discussing the Constitution. In politics, being conservative doesn't mean you have to wear a tie and a stuffy suit, just as progressive doesn't have to pertain to progress. To be a conservative means to conserve the original values of the Constitution. To be progressive means your stance progresses away from those original values. It's simple, but a lot of people don't recognize the difference in meaning.

In 1936, Senator Millard Tydings of Maryland introduced a resolution in Congress calling for a constitutional amendment to require a balanced federal budget. Tydings' proposal reflected the growing unease about federal spending during the New Deal era, as President Franklin D. Roosevelt's administration had dramatically expanded government programs to combat the Great Depression. Opponents of Roosevelt's policies, especially fiscal conservatives, feared that the burgeoning federal debt would lead to long-term economic instability.

Although Tydings' proposal did not gain significant traction, it set the stage for future debates. During this period, Keynesian economics—which advocated for government intervention in the economy, particularly through deficit spending during recessions—began to take hold in the United States. The Keynesian argument that deficits could be beneficial during economic downturns became a central tenet of opposition to a balanced budget amendment.

The 1970s: The Rise of the Balanced Budget Movement

The movement for a balanced budget amendment gained new momentum in the 1970s, driven largely by concerns over rising inflation, growing federal deficits, and increasing national debt. The economic challenges of the 1970s, including the oil crises and stagflation, led many Americans to question the government's fiscal policies.

In 1975, Senator Walter Mondale and Congressman Richard Gephardt, both Democrats, introduced a resolution in Congress to require a balanced budget. Their proposal reflected the bipartisan nature of early efforts to impose fiscal discipline on the federal government. Unlike today's political climate, these Democrats were open to collaborating with Republicans on ideas that benefited the country. However, their initiative faced substantial opposition, particularly from liberals who feared that a constitutional amendment would hamper the government's ability to respond to economic crises and fund essential social programs.

Around this time, grassroots efforts to advance a balanced budget amendment began to take shape. Conservative organizations like the National Taxpayers Union and libertarian groups pushed for states to call for a constitutional convention to pass a BBA. Under Article V of the U.S. Constitution, a constitutional convention can be convened if two-thirds of state legislatures request it, bypassing Congress. By 1979, 30 state legislatures had passed resolutions calling for such a convention to propose a balanced budget amendment, falling just four states short of the required threshold.

Despite growing support, the movement stalled as concerns about the unpredictability of a constitutional convention and its potential consequences mounted. Critics warned that a convention could lead to a wide-ranging overhaul of the Constitution, raising fears among liberals and moderates alike.

The Reagan Era: The Push for Fiscal Responsibility

The election of President Ronald Reagan in 1980 brought renewed focus to the issue of fiscal responsibility. Reagan, a staunch advocate of smaller government and lower taxes, campaigned on a platform of reducing the size of the federal government and balancing the budget. However, despite Reagan's rhetorical commitment to fiscal conservatism, his administration oversaw a dramatic increase in federal deficits, driven in part by his large tax cuts and increased defense spending.

During Reagan's presidency, a balanced budget amendment became a prominent feature of conservative policy discussions. In 1982, the Senate Judiciary Committee approved a proposed balanced budget amendment that would have required the federal government to balance its budget every year, except in cases of national emergency or war. The proposal garnered widespread support among Republicans and fiscal conservatives, but it faced fierce opposition from Democrats and liberal interest groups.

Critics of the amendment argued that it would severely limit the government's ability to respond to economic downturns and emergencies. They pointed to the potential harm that could result from forcing the government to cut spending or raise taxes during a recession, which could exacerbate economic problems rather than solve them. Paul Samuelson, a Nobel laureate in economics, described the idea of a balanced budget amendment as "economic illiteracy," arguing that it would tie the government's hands during times of crisis.

Despite passing the Senate with a narrow majority in 1982, the Balanced Budget Amendment failed to achieve the two-thirds majority required to move forward. The proposal continued to be a subject of debate throughout the 1980s, but it never gained the political momentum necessary for passage.

The 1990s: The Balanced Budget Debate Reaches Its Peak

The 1990s witnessed the most serious efforts to pass a balanced budget amendment in the United States. By this time, the federal deficit had become a central issue in American politics. President George H.W. Bush faced significant criticism for failing to balance the budget, and his decision to break his famous "no new taxes" pledge further alienated fiscal conservatives.

The election of Bill Clinton in 1992, followed by the Republican Contract with America in 1994, reinvigorated the push for a balanced budget amendment. Led by Newt Gingrich, the newly Republican-controlled Congress made the passage of a balanced budget amendment one of its top priorities. In 1995, the House of Representatives passed the Balanced Budget Amendment by a wide margin, marking the first time in history that such a measure had passed a chamber of Congress.

The debate then moved to the Senate, where it became the focus of intense political and ideological struggle. Supporters argued that the amendment was necessary to impose fiscal discipline on Congress and prevent future generations from being saddled with insurmountable debt. They pointed to the success of many states that had implemented balanced budget requirements at the state level and argued that similar constraints should be placed on the federal government.

Opponents, including many Democrats and some moderate Republicans, raised concerns about the potential consequences of a balanced budget amendment. They argued that the amendment would force cuts to essential programs like Social Security and Medicare, and that it would hinder the government's ability to respond to economic downturns. The debate became deeply partisan, with Republicans largely in favor of the amendment and Democrats largely opposed.

In March 1995, the Senate came within one vote of passing the Balanced Budget Amendment, falling short of the required two-thirds majority by a margin of 65-35. The amendment's failure was a devastating blow to fiscal conservatives, but it underscored the growing urgency of the balanced budget issue in American politics.

The Modern Era: Renewed Calls Amidst Growing Debt

In the years since the near-passage of the Balanced Budget Amendment in the 1990s, the issue has continued to resurface, though it has never gained the same level of momentum. The early 2000s saw a temporary decline in the national deficit, with the U.S. government achieving budget surpluses under President Bill Clinton from 1998 to 2001. However, the fiscal discipline achieved during this period was short-lived, as the Bush tax cuts, increased military spending in the aftermath of the 9/11 attacks, and the War on Terror drove the federal deficit back up.

The war on Terror and its associated costs, combined with the financial crisis of 2007–2008, significantly increased the national debt and reignited discussions about fiscal responsibility and the need for a balanced budget amendment.

During President George W. Bush's administration, the national debt grew substantially, sparking criticism from fiscal conservatives who felt that the government had lost control of its spending. The national debt exceeded $10 trillion by the end of Bush's presidency, largely driven by tax cuts, increased military spending, and the costs associated with the Medicare prescription drug benefit.

In the wake of the 2008 financial crisis, the federal government's fiscal response, which included bailouts for financial institutions and the American Recovery and Reinvestment Act under President Barack Obama, further swelled the deficit. By 2010, the national debt had reached over $14 trillion, and the annual federal budget deficit hit unprecedented levels.

These developments provided renewed urgency for those advocating for a balanced budget amendment. Conservatives and deficit hawks called for a constitutional amendment as the only way to prevent what they saw as unsustainable spending patterns. However, the political landscape had shifted, and the partisan divide over fiscal policy had deepened, making bipartisan cooperation on the issue more difficult than in previous decades.

The Tea Party Movement and Renewed Efforts

The Tea Party movement, which emerged in 2009 as a response to the Obama administration's spending policies, brought the issue of the national debt and deficits back into the spotlight. Tea Party activists were strongly in favor of a balanced budget amendment and demanded that Congress take serious action to reduce federal spending.

In 2011, during the negotiations over raising the federal debt ceiling, the House of Representatives, led by Speaker John Boehner and bolstered by newly elected Tea Party Republicans, once again pushed for a balanced budget amendment as part of a broader package of fiscal reforms. The Republican-controlled House passed a balanced budget amendment in November 2011, but it failed to gain the necessary two-thirds majority in the Senate.

This failure reignited a fierce political debate. Advocates of the BBA argued that without a constitutional requirement, Congress would never have the discipline to control spending. They contended that the skyrocketing national debt posed a grave threat to the economic stability and future prosperity of the United States. Additionally, proponents highlighted the success of states that had implemented balanced budget requirements and argued that it was time for the federal government to follow suit.

Opponents, primarily Democrats and some moderate Republicans, continued to resist. They held to their argument that a rigid requirement to balance the budget would handcuff the government in times of economic crises, natural disasters, or national emergencies. They also contended that such an amendment could force severe cuts to essential programs, including Social Security, Medicare, and defense spending. Many also pointed out that deficit spending had historically been necessary during times of war or economic downturns, such as the Great Depression and World War II, to stimulate the economy and protect national security.

The 2011 effort to pass a balanced budget amendment, like earlier attempts, ultimately failed due to a combination of political opposition and concerns over its potential economic consequences. However, the debate over the BBA was far from over, as fiscal conservatives vowed to continue their fight.

The National Debt Crisis and Rising Public Concern

The 2010s saw a steady increase in public concern over the national debt. As of March 2025, the U.S. national debt has exceeded $36 trillion, with annual budget deficits consistently adding to this total. The causes are multifaceted, including tax cuts, entitlement program costs, defense spending, and, most recently, the response to the COVID-19 pandemic, which saw trillions of dollars in government spending aimed at stabilizing the economy. I think it's important to put numbers into context. When I was a kid, I used to think a million was a lot. When the government started talking using figures in the billions, people would always clarify, "Yes, that's billions with a B." These days, we throw around figures in the billions so often that I think the majority of the public has been desensitized and may not have a full grasp of just how much a trillion is. For example, if you started spending a million dollars every single day since Jesus was born, you still wouldn't have spent a trillion dollars. Another mathematician puts it like this: "1 million seconds is about 11.5 days, 1 billion seconds is about 32 years, while a trillion seconds is equal to 32,000 years." Let that sink in.

As deficits and debt levels have risen, public opinion has become more divided. Polls indicate that many Americans express concern over the growing national debt, but there remains substantial disagreement on how to address it. While fiscal conservatives and libertarians have consistently supported a BBA as a solution, many progressives and centrists argue for a more flexible approach to fiscal policy, one that allows for deficit spending in times of economic need.

The national debt has also become a key issue in political campaigns. In recent elections, many candidates for Congress and the presidency have promised to reduce the debt and balance the budget, though few have succeeded in achieving these goals. The difficulty lies in reconciling the public's demand for both fiscal responsibility and the continuation of popular government programs.

Opposition to the Balanced Budget Amendment: Arguments and Concerns

Opposition to a balanced budget amendment has been consistent throughout its history, with critics arguing that such a measure could create more problems than it solves. There are several key arguments against the BBA that have been raised by economists, political leaders, and interest groups over the decades.

A. Flexibility in Economic Crises

One of the most prominent arguments against a BBA is that it would remove the government's ability to respond effectively to economic crises. Keynesian economists argue that deficit spending is crucial during recessions and depressions because it stimulates demand and helps the economy recover. If the government were required to balance the budget during a downturn, it might be forced to cut spending or raise taxes, both of which could exacerbate the economic problems rather than solving them.

For example, during the Great Recession of 2008–2009, the federal government engaged in significant deficit spending to stabilize the economy. The stimulus package, known as the American Recovery and Reinvestment Act, was widely credited with preventing a deeper economic collapse. Critics of a BBA argue that such actions would have been impossible under a constitutional requirement to balance the budget.

B. Impact on Social Programs

Another major concern is that a BBA would force cuts to essential government programs, particularly entitlement programs like Social Security, Medicare, and Medicaid. These programs make up a significant portion of the federal budget, and balancing the budget without touching them would be extremely difficult. Many critics argue that a BBA could disproportionately hurt low-income Americans and seniors who rely on these programs for financial security.

Opponents also argue that defense spending, infrastructure, and education could be slashed under a BBA, as lawmakers would be forced to find ways to cut expenditures to meet the constitutional requirement.

C. Legal and Political Complexity

A balanced budget amendment could also lead to legal and political complications. If Congress were to pass a BBA, it might require courts to intervene in budgetary matters, a role traditionally reserved for the legislative and executive branches. Some legal scholars have argued that enforcing a balanced budget would be difficult, and disputes over whether the budget was truly balanced could lead to lengthy legal battles.

Additionally, the amendment could result in political gridlock, as lawmakers grapple with difficult decisions about where to cut spending or how to raise revenue. These challenges could exacerbate partisan divides and make the legislative process even more dysfunctional.

D. Potential for Economic Harm

Finally, critics argue that a balanced budget amendment could do more harm than good by forcing the government to make short-term decisions at the expense of long-term economic health. A rigid requirement to balance the budget might discourage investment in infrastructure, research, and education—areas that require significant upfront costs but generate long-term economic benefits.

The Case for a Balanced Budget Amendment

Despite these objections, proponents of a balanced budget amendment argue that the benefits far outweigh the potential drawbacks. The primary argument in favor of a BBA is that it would impose much-needed fiscal discipline on Congress, which has consistently failed to manage the nation's finances responsibly. With the national debt now exceeding $36 trillion, proponents contend that the federal government is on an unsustainable fiscal trajectory that threatens the nation's economic future.

A. Preventing Reckless Spending

Supporters argue that a BBA would force lawmakers to make difficult but necessary decisions about spending priorities. Without the ability to borrow endlessly, Congress would be required to balance the budget and live within its means, just as families and businesses do. Proponents believe this would help eliminate wasteful government programs, reduce corruption, and prevent the kind of deficit spending that has led to the current debt crisis.

B. Promoting Long-Term Stability

A BBA, its supporters argue, would promote long-term economic stability by preventing the government from engaging in unsustainable borrowing practices. By requiring balanced budgets, the government would be forced to make fiscally responsible decisions that would benefit future generations. Proponents contend that this would lead to a stronger, more stable economy over the long term, with lower inflation and greater financial security for Americans.

C. Public Support and Political Accountability

Proponents also note that a balanced budget amendment has broad public support. Polls consistently show that a majority of Americans believe the government should be required to balance its budget. Advocates argue that passing a BBA would help restore public trust in the federal government by demonstrating that lawmakers are serious about addressing the national debt.

Moreover, a BBA could increase political accountability by making it clear to voters when lawmakers are violating fiscal discipline. If a constitutional requirement for a balanced budget were in place, elected officials would be held accountable for any failure to meet that requirement, giving voters a stronger role in ensuring responsible governance.

Conclusion: The Path Forward

The history of proposed balanced budget amendments in the United States reflects a long-standing and contentious debate over the proper role of government in managing the nation's finances. While numerous efforts to pass a BBA have failed, the issue remains as relevant as ever in the face of rising deficits and mounting national debt.

For proponents, the case for a balanced budget amendment is clear: without a constitutional requirement to balance the budget, Congress will continue to engage in reckless spending and burden future generations with insurmountable debt. A BBA would force lawmakers to make difficult decisions about spending, prioritize essential services, and impose the fiscal discipline that is sorely lacking in the current political system. They argue that without such a safeguard, the federal government will continue to live beyond its means, leading to long-term economic instability and a diminished future for the next generation of Americans.

11. Learning from State-Level Successes

Proponents of a balanced budget amendment often point to the success of similar measures at the state level. Currently, 49 out of 50 U.S. states have some form of balanced budget requirement for their state governments, though the exact rules and enforcement mechanisms vary. These requirements have generally forced states to keep their spending in line with revenues, ensuring that deficits do not spiral out of control.

For example, states like Texas and Colorado are often cited as examples of fiscal responsibility, where balanced budget mandates have led to more prudent financial practices. These states, proponents argue, provide a blueprint for what could be achieved at the federal level with a similar constitutional requirement. While opponents often argue that the federal government's role is far more complex than that of individual states—particularly in terms of defense spending, social programs, and responding to national emergencies—supporters of a BBA contend that the principle remains the same: the government should not spend money it doesn't have.

Safeguards for Flexibility: Designing a Realistic BBA

One of the most common criticisms of a balanced budget amendment is the concern that it could overly constrain the government in times of crisis, such as during wars, recessions, or natural disasters. Proponents of a BBA acknowledge this concern and have proposed several safeguards to ensure that a BBA would not cripple the government's ability to respond effectively to emergencies.

A. Emergency Exemptions

Most versions of a proposed balanced budget amendment include provisions for emergencies. For example, the BBA could allow for deficits in cases of war, economic downturns, or other national emergencies, but only with the approval of a supermajority in Congress. This would ensure that deficit spending could still occur when absolutely necessary, but it would prevent the kind of routine deficit spending that has become the norm in Washington.

Such an exemption would require a high threshold—such as a two-thirds vote in both the House and Senate—to authorize deficit spending, ensuring that any such decision would be made with broad bipartisan support. This would prevent the misuse of emergency powers and ensure that deficit spending is truly reserved for times of national need.

B. Economic Triggers

Another potential safeguard could involve economic triggers. For instance, a BBA could include provisions that allow for limited deficit spending when the economy is in a recession, as measured by specific economic indicators such as unemployment rates or GDP growth. This would allow the government to use fiscal policy to stimulate the economy during downturns without abandoning the long-term goal of fiscal responsibility.

By including such flexibility, a balanced budget amendment could be designed in a way that promotes fiscal responsibility during periods of normal economic growth while still allowing the government to act decisively during times of economic hardship.

C. Phased Implementation

To ease the transition to a balanced budget amendment, some proposals have suggested implementing the amendment gradually over several years. This phased approach would allow the federal government time to adjust its spending priorities and reform entitlement programs without causing a sudden shock to the economy.

For example, a BBA could require a reduction in the deficit over a set period—say, five to ten years—before achieving full balance. This would give lawmakers time to make necessary reforms and adjustments, allowing for a smoother and more deliberate transition to a balanced budget without risking immediate economic disruption.

The Long-Term Case for a Balanced Budget Amendment

The United States is currently facing unprecedented levels of debt, and many economists agree that without serious fiscal reforms, the country is on a dangerous trajectory. The national debt, now over $36 trillion as of this writing and increases by about $1 million every 20 seconds. It represents not only a burden on future generations but also a significant threat to the country's economic stability. Rising interest payments on the debt are crowding out other spending priorities, and the growing debt load risks undermining investor confidence in the U.S. economy.

Proponents of a balanced budget amendment argue that the current path is unsustainable and only a constitutional amendment can force the changes needed to put the nation back on sound fiscal footing. They point to the failure of Congress to enact meaningful spending reforms or deficit reduction measures in recent decades, despite repeated promises from both political parties.

A balanced budget amendment, they argue, would create a legal obligation to balance the budget, preventing Congress from continuing to defer difficult decisions. It would impose a level of discipline that has been lacking in Washington, forcing lawmakers to confront the reality that the government cannot spend more than it takes in without incurring serious long-term consequences.

A. Reducing the National Debt

Proponents of a BBA believe that a constitutional amendment is the only way to truly rein in government spending and begin the process of reducing the debt. They argue that without a firm legal requirement to balance the budget, Congress will continue to rely on borrowing to fund government programs, ultimately leaving future generations to pay the price.

A balanced budget amendment would force lawmakers to prioritize debt reduction as a key policy goal. By limiting the government's ability to run deficits, the amendment would require the federal government to gradually pay down its debt, ultimately leading to a more sustainable fiscal policy. When interest rates increase, the cost of servicing the national debt rises because a significant portion of government debt is issued in the form of bonds, such as Treasury bills, notes, and bonds. These bonds pay interest to investors, and as rates go up, the government must offer higher yields to attract buyers when issuing new debt or rolling over existing debt. In short, rising interest rates directly increase the cost of maintaining the national debt, reducing the government's ability to spend on other priorities and potentially leading to greater fiscal challenges.

B. Restoring Trust in Government

Also in favor of a balanced budget amendment is that it would help restore public trust in government. Many Americans are deeply frustrated by what they perceive as irresponsible government spending and the accumulation of unsustainable debt. A balanced budget amendment would signal a commitment to fiscal responsibility and long-term economic health, potentially restoring confidence in the government's ability to manage the nation's finances.

A BBA would also create a more transparent and accountable budgeting process. With a legal requirement to balance the budget, Congress would be forced to make tough decisions about where to allocate resources, leading to a more open debate about spending priorities. This could help reduce the influence of special interest groups and ensure that taxpayer dollars are spent more efficiently.

The Road Ahead: Building Support for a Balanced Budget Amendment

Despite numerous attempts over the years, a balanced budget amendment has yet to be added to the U.S. Constitution. However, proponents remain determined, believing that the growing national debt and persistent budget deficits will eventually create the political will necessary to pass such an amendment.

To achieve this goal, supporters of a BBA will need to build broad bipartisan support. While the issue of fiscal responsibility resonates most strongly with conservatives, there is potential for a bipartisan coalition to form around the idea of a balanced budget amendment. Many moderate Democrats and independents are also concerned about the national debt and may be open to supporting a BBA if it includes safeguards for social programs and flexibility during economic crises.

Proponents will also need to engage the public in the debate. Polls show that a majority of Americans support the idea of a balanced budget amendment, but the issue has not always been a top priority for voters. By highlighting the long-term consequences of the national debt and the potential benefits of a BBA, advocates can help build the public pressure necessary to compel lawmakers to act.

Conclusion: A Balanced Budget Amendment as a Path to Fiscal Responsibility

The history of balanced budget amendment proposals in the United States is a testament to the enduring debate over how best to manage the nation's finances. While numerous attempts to pass a BBA have failed, the issue remains a critical one as the country faces rising debt and persistent budget deficits.

Proponents of a balanced budget amendment argue that such a measure is necessary to impose fiscal discipline on Congress and prevent the government from engaging in reckless deficit spending. By forcing lawmakers to balance the budget, the amendment would help reduce the national debt, promote long-term economic stability, and restore public trust in government.

While there are legitimate concerns about the potential consequences of a BBA, many of these concerns can be addressed through careful design, including emergency exemptions and economic triggers. With the right safeguards in place, a balanced budget amendment could provide the fiscal discipline needed to secure the nation's economic future while still allowing the government the flexibility to respond to crises.

As the national debt continues to grow, the case for a balanced budget amendment becomes ever more compelling. For the sake of future generations, it may be time for the United States to finally adopt this long-debated constitutional reform and put the nation on a more sustainable fiscal path.

5

ZERO-BASE BUDGETING: A PATH TO FISCAL RESPONSIBILITY

A S THE UNITED STATES GRAPPLES WITH escalating national debt and fiscal mismanagement, innovative solutions are essential to restore economic stability and ensure the government operates efficiently. One such solution is zero-base budgeting (ZBB), a budgeting method that requires each department or agency to justify every expense, starting from zero, rather than relying on previous budget figures as the baseline. This approach encourages a detailed re-evaluation of spending priorities and aligns resources with actual needs rather than incremental growth. In this chapter, I will present the case for adopting zero-base budgeting as a key component of broader fiscal reforms. I will explore the benefits of ZBB, including increased transparency, accountability, and financial discipline. I will also examine the arguments against zero-base budgeting, recognizing the challenges and limitations it may pose, while arguing that, despite these concerns, ZBB represents a crucial tool for reigning in government spending and making more informed decisions about resource allocation.

Understanding Zero-Base Budgeting

Zero-base budgeting is a budgeting approach that requires all expenses to be justified for each new period, beginning with a "zero base." Unlike traditional budgeting, which uses the previous year's budget as a starting point and adds or subtracts from it, ZBB forces departments to start from scratch, scrutinizing every dollar they request. The aim is to ensure that every program or expenditure has a clear purpose and delivers value to the public.

The process of zero-base budgeting typically involves:

1. **Identifying decision units:** Each department, agency, or program is treated as a decision unit, responsible for justifying its existence and funding needs.
2. **Building cost-effective alternatives:** Each unit presents various spending levels, from bare minimum to optimal, allowing decision-makers to weigh alternatives.
3. **Ranking priorities:** Leaders assess the importance of each program, rank them based on necessity and efficiency, and allocate resources accordingly.

This method, originally developed in the private sector by **Peter Pyhrr** at Texas Instruments in the 1970s, gained attention in public finance as a way to curb unnecessary government spending.

The Case for Zero-Base Budgeting

A. Eliminating Wasteful Spending

One of the most compelling arguments for zero-base budgeting is its ability to identify and eliminate wasteful spending. Traditional budgeting often encourages "budgetary inertia," where departments receive automatic increases year after year, regardless of performance or actual needs. This incremental approach creates inefficiencies, with programs continuing to receive funding without rigorous evaluation.

ZBB forces each department to justify its expenditures based on current needs and performance, not past allocations. By scrutinizing every program, leaders can cut funding to underperforming or obsolete initiatives, ensuring that taxpayer dollars are directed toward high-priority areas. For a government facing trillions in debt, this kind of comprehensive review is long overdue.

B. Enhancing Accountability and Transparency

Zero-base budgeting promotes greater **accountability** by making every department responsible for justifying its existence and expenditures. Rather than simply requesting more funds each year, agencies must demonstrate why they need the money and how they plan to use it effectively. This process brings a higher level of scrutiny to government spending, helping to expose inefficiencies and mismanagement.

Moreover, ZBB fosters **transparency** in government operations. Since all programs are evaluated from the ground up, the public can see where and how their tax dollars are being spent. This level of transparency is critical to restoring public trust in government, especially at a time when many Americans feel that their leaders are not being good stewards of the nation's finances.

C. Flexibility and Adaptability

In a rapidly changing world, government spending priorities must be flexible enough to adapt to new challenges. Whether responding to a public health crisis, national security threat, or technological innovation, the federal budget needs to reflect current realities.

Zero-base budgeting allows for this kind of flexibility by requiring departments to re-evaluate their needs every year.

It encourages innovation and adaptability, as agencies must consider alternative ways of achieving their objectives and be ready to adjust their spending in response to changing circumstances.

For instance, during the **COVID-19 pandemic**, the federal government had to quickly allocate funds for healthcare, economic relief, and vaccine distribution. A traditional budgeting approach might have been too slow to respond to such an urgent situation. ZBB, with its built-in capacity for re-prioritizing spending, could help the government pivot resources more effectively in the face of emerging challenges.

D. Promoting Efficient Use of Resources

At its core, zero-base budgeting emphasizes **efficiency**. By forcing departments to justify every dollar, ZBB encourages a more careful and thoughtful allocation of resources. It discourages the common practice of "use-it-or-lose-it" spending, where departments rush to spend their remaining budget near the end of the fiscal year to avoid cuts in future budgets.

With ZBB, the focus shifts to optimizing the use of resources, aligning funding with actual needs rather than arbitrary increases. This makes it possible to allocate funds where they are truly needed, such as critical infrastructure projects, defense, education, or healthcare, while trimming down bloated or redundant programs.

E. Better Long-Term Financial Planning

Adopting zero-base budgeting would improve **long-term financial planning** for the government. Since ZBB requires a comprehensive review of each department's goals and expenditures, it encourages a longer-term perspective on government spending. Agencies are incentivized to focus on the outcomes of their programs and their contributions to broader national goals, such as economic growth, national security, or public health.

This shift from short-term, incremental budget increases to a results-oriented, performance-based approach can lead to more sustainable financial practices. By scrutinizing the necessity and efficiency of programs, ZBB helps prevent the accumulation of unsustainable debt over time, promoting fiscal responsibility and accountability to future generations.

Addressing Criticisms of Zero-Base Budgeting

Despite the numerous advantages of zero-base budgeting, critics argue that the method has its drawbacks. These criticisms often center around its practicality, resource demands, and potential disruption to government operations. It is essential to acknowledge these concerns while making the case that, with the right implementation, ZBB can be a powerful tool for reform.

A. Resource-Intensive Process

One of the most common criticisms of zero-base budgeting is that it is **resource intensive.** Unlike traditional budgeting, which builds on prior year allocations, ZBB requires a comprehensive review of every department's budget from scratch. This process involves gathering extensive data, preparing detailed justifications, and considering multiple alternative spending levels for each program. Critics argue that this can be both time-consuming and expensive, placing a significant burden on government agencies already stretched thin.

However, proponents of ZBB argue that the upfront investment of time and resources is outweighed by the long-term benefits of more efficient spending. While ZBB may require more effort than traditional budgeting, the potential savings from eliminating waste and improving resource allocation could far exceed these costs. In the private sector, companies that have adopted ZBB have reported significant cost reductions—anywhere from 10% to 25%—by cutting non-essential spending. Similar results could be achieved in government with a commitment to the process.

B. Potential for Bureaucratic Resistance

Government agencies accustomed to receiving incremental budget increases may resist the adoption of zero-base budgeting. Bureaucracies often operate with established norms and processes, and any significant disruption to these norms can lead to pushback. Critics argue that the re-evaluation of every expenditure could face bureaucratic resistance, with agencies reluctant to expose inefficiencies or risk losing funding for programs they deem essential.

While this is a valid concern, proponents of ZBB argue that it can be addressed through strong leadership and clear communication. If the adoption of zero-base budgeting is part of a broader effort to promote fiscal responsibility and transparency, and if leaders in government emphasize the importance of accountability, agencies will have a stronger incentive to comply. Moreover, the long-term benefits of ZBB—such as the potential for better outcomes and improved public trust—can help mitigate resistance.

C. Risk of Over-Simplification

Some critics argue that zero-base budgeting could lead to an **over-simplified view** of government programs. Not all government functions can easily be quantified or justified in the same way, and certain programs may deliver intangible benefits that are difficult to measure through a strict ZBB approach. For example, programs related to public health, environmental protection, or social welfare may not show immediate economic returns but could have significant long-term benefits for society.

However, proponents of ZBB contend that this is more of a challenge in execution rather than an inherent flaw in the system. ZBB can and should be adapted to account for qualitative factors, particularly when evaluating programs that provide indirect or long-term societal benefits. The key is to establish clear criteria for evaluation and to ensure that decision-makers consider both quantitative and qualitative outcomes when ranking budget priorities.

D. Short-Term Focus vs. Long-Term Goals

Another concern is that zero-base budgeting, by focusing on justifying each year's expenditures, might lead to a **short-term focus** at the expense of long-term goals. Critics fear that agencies, in their effort to justify their immediate funding, may deprioritize long-term investments that do not yield immediate results but are crucial for future growth and stability.

In response, proponents of ZBB argue that the method can be designed to incorporate long-term planning. By requiring agencies to justify their budgets based on long-term outcomes and performance metrics, ZBB can encourage a more strategic approach to spending. Furthermore, incorporating multi-year budget cycles into the ZBB process could help balance short-term needs with long-term objectives, ensuring that investments in infrastructure, research, and development are not neglected.

Why Zero-Base Budgeting is Right for America Today

In an era of unprecedented government debt and fiscal challenges, the United States needs bold and innovative reforms to bring fiscal responsibility back to the forefront of governance. Zero-base budgeting (ZBB) offers a solution that aligns with the pressing need to **curb runaway spending, reduce inefficiencies**, and restore public trust in how tax dollars are managed. While critics raise valid concerns about the resource demands and bureaucratic resistance that could accompany ZBB, the potential benefits—such as **eliminating waste**, **enhancing transparency**, and fostering a more **accountable government**—far outweigh these challenges. In fact, the case for adopting ZBB today is stronger than ever.

A. Addressing the National Debt Crisis

The most urgent reason for implementing zero-base budgeting is the rising **national debt**, which has surpassed $36 trillion as of 2025. This mounting debt represents a looming crisis that threatens the long-term financial health of the country, burdening future generations with interest payments that crowd out critical investments in infrastructure, education, and healthcare. The conventional approach to budgeting—where previous spending levels are used as a baseline—has contributed to the accumulation of this debt by encouraging unchecked increases year after year, regardless of actual needs or performance.

Zero-base budgeting breaks this cycle by forcing lawmakers to rethink spending from the ground up. Every dollar spent must be justified, and departments must compete for funding based on merit and efficiency, rather than relying on past allocations. This shift could help the U.S. government begin to reverse the trend of deficit spending, paving the way for a more sustainable fiscal future.

B. Aligning Spending with National Priorities

In the current budgetary process, programs that may no longer serve the nation's most pressing needs often continue to receive funding, while newer, more urgent priorities struggle for resources. For instance, the rapid rise of **cybersecurity threats** and **climate change** has created new challenges that demand government attention and funding. However, the existing budgetary system often prioritizes legacy programs that may no longer be effective or necessary.

Zero-based budgeting offers the flexibility to **redirect resources** where they are needed most. By evaluating every program based on its current relevance and performance, ZBB enables decision-makers to align the budget with **evolving national priorities**. This ensures that government spending reflects the changing needs of the nation, rather than perpetuating outdated allocations.

C. Empowering Policymakers and Citizens

Another significant benefit of ZBB is its potential to **empower policymakers** to make more informed decisions. Rather than simply accepting budget proposals based on incremental changes, lawmakers would have a clearer picture of the costs and benefits of each program. This transparency would lead to more **constructive debates** about spending priorities, helping Congress focus on what truly matters to constituents.

Moreover, zero-base budgeting could enhance **citizen engagement** in the budgeting process. By making the process more transparent and understandable, ZBB allows voters to see exactly how their tax dollars are being spent and hold elected officials accountable for wasteful or unnecessary expenditures. In this way, ZBB fosters a stronger connection between the government and the people, which is essential for a healthy democracy.

Learning from Success Stories

Several states and private sector organizations have successfully implemented forms of zero-base budgeting, providing valuable lessons for how the federal government could adopt this approach. **Georgia** and **Texas** are notable examples of states that have employed ZBB at various points to improve fiscal management.

A. Georgia's Experience with Zero-Base Budgeting

In 2012, the state of **Georgia** introduced a modified version of zero-base budgeting under then-Governor **Nathan Deal**. The goal was to review state programs systematically and ensure that each dollar spent delivered measurable value. Georgia's ZBB process targeted specific areas of the state budget for review each year, allowing for a thorough evaluation of expenditures while avoiding the burden of a full-scale ZBB overhaul annually.

The results were positive: Georgia was able to **identify savings**, eliminate redundancies, and streamline programs, leading to a more efficient use of state resources. One of the key takeaways from Georgia's experience is that ZBB can be successfully tailored to focus on high-priority areas while still delivering significant benefits in terms of cost savings and accountability.

B. The Private Sector and ZBB

The private sector has also provided numerous examples of the successful implementation of ZBB. Companies like **3G Capital** and **Kraft Heinz** have used zero-base budgeting to reduce operational costs and improve profitability. By forcing managers to justify every expense, these companies have identified and eliminated wasteful spending, redirected resources to high-impact areas, and improved overall financial health.

While the goals of the private sector differ from those of government, the fundamental principles of ZBB—scrutinizing expenditures, eliminating inefficiencies, and aligning resources with priorities—are highly transferable to the public sector. The success of ZBB in the business world demonstrates its potential to drive meaningful change in government budgeting as well.

Responding to Critics: Addressing the Practical Challenges

As with any significant reform, implementing zero-base budgeting at the federal level would present practical challenges. Critics often point to the **complexity** and **resource intensity** of ZBB, suggesting that it may be impractical to apply it across the entire federal government. However, these concerns can be mitigated through careful design and phased implementation.

A. Phased Implementation for Practicality

One way to address the resource demands of ZBB is through a **phased approach**. Instead of applying zero-base budgeting to every department at once, the federal government could begin by focusing on high-impact areas, such as discretionary spending, or specific agencies where wasteful spending is suspected. Over time, the scope of ZBB could expand, allowing the government to implement the process gradually and avoid overwhelming departments with new demands.

By starting with a targeted approach, policymakers can build capacity within agencies to handle the ZBB process and demonstrate the benefits of the method before scaling up. This phased implementation would also allow the government to **refine** the process and address any challenges that arise along the way.

B. Leveraging Technology for Efficiency

Another way to reduce the complexity of zero-base budgeting is by leveraging **modern technology** to streamline the process. Data analytics tools, performance-tracking systems, and automation can simplify the collection and analysis of budgetary information, making it easier for departments to justify their expenditures and for decision-makers to evaluate them.

The use of technology would reduce the administrative burden on government agencies, enabling them to focus on evaluating the effectiveness of their programs rather than getting bogged down in manual data collection. By incorporating advanced tools into the ZBB process, the government can reduce costs and improve the efficiency of budget management.

C. Encouraging a Culture Shift

Lastly, successfully implementing zero-base budgeting requires a **cultural shift** within government agencies. Instead of viewing budget increases as a given, agencies need to adopt a mindset of **fiscal responsibility** and **performance-based budgeting**. This shift will take time and leadership, but it is crucial to ensure that ZBB delivers its intended results.

Through education, training, and strong leadership, government agencies can transition toward a culture that prioritizes **efficient resource use** and **accountability**. By demonstrating the benefits of zero-base budgeting—such as improved outcomes, greater flexibility, and better use of taxpayer dollars—policymakers can build support for this transformative approach.

Conclusion: The Need for Bold Action

Clearly, traditional budgeting methods have failed to deliver the fiscal discipline necessary for long-term stability. **Zero-base budgeting** represents a bold, forward-thinking solution that can help the government regain control of its finances, eliminate waste, and allocate resources where they are truly needed.

Challenges can be addressed through phased implementation, the use of technology, and a cultural shift toward fiscal responsibility. In fact, the potential benefits of ZBB—enhanced transparency, accountability, flexibility, and efficiency—make it a compelling option for reforming government budgeting in the 21st century.

Zero-base budgeting is not a magic bullet that will solve all of the nation's fiscal problems overnight. However, it is a critical tool that, when combined with other reforms, can help steer the United States back onto a sustainable fiscal path. By embracing ZBB, policymakers can ensure that every dollar spent by the government delivers real value, helping to restore public trust and secure a better future for all Americans.

6

ELECTION INTEGRITY – SECURING DEMOCRACY THROUGH COMMON-SENSE REFORMS

E LECTION INTEGRITY IS THE CORNERSTONE OF a functioning democracy. Without it, the public's faith in the democratic process erodes, and the legitimacy of elected officials comes into question. Unfortunately, in recent years, concerns over election security and fairness have intensified. The introduction of new technologies and expanded voting methods—while aimed at making voting more accessible—have also raised questions about the transparency and security of our elections.

The 2020 U.S. presidential election saw an unprecedented expansion of mail-in voting due to the COVID-19 pandemic, raising concerns among some about potential voter fraud. Critics argued that the large-scale use of mail-in ballots increased the risk of fraud, citing vulnerabilities like ballot harvesting, inaccurate voter rolls, and the potential for unauthorized individuals to cast votes. **"True the Vote"** is a conservative organization focused on election integrity and voter fraud prevention in the United States. Founded in 2009 by **Catherine Engelbrecht**, the group advocates for stricter voter ID laws, maintaining accurate voter rolls, and increasing oversight at polling places. "True The Vote" did an extensive job of uncovering election fraud by tracking what they call "mules" through cell phone data. The mules were tracked going back and forth between non-governmental agencies and drop boxes repeatedly. The video images of these mules stuffing hundreds and even thousands of ballots into boxes are enough to raise eyebrows, but not one judge wanted to hear the evidence, most citing a standing issue.

When a judge denies a case on standing, it means the court has determined that the party bringing the lawsuit does not have the legal right to do so. Standing is a legal principle that ensures only individuals or groups directly affected by an issue can bring a case to court.

The 2022 film *2000 Mules* brought these incidences to light but faced significant criticism from election "experts," "fact-checkers," and mainstream "media outlets" for lacking solid evidence and for making speculative and misleading claims that include:

1. **No Evidence of Widespread Fraud:** *Independent investigations by state election officials, the Department of Justice, and courts have not found any evidence of widespread voter fraud in the 2020 election, including any organized ballot-harvesting operations.*
   However, as I mentioned, almost every judge ruled that the parties filing the claims had no standing. This prevented anyone from presenting any evidence to the contrary.

2. **Geolocation Data Limitations:** *Experts in geolocation data analysis have pointed out that simply tracking a person's movement via cell phone data does not prove illegal activity. People might pass by or visit drop boxes for legitimate reasons without engaging in fraud.*

While this answer may be designed to keep people off the scent on a good trail, it doesn't address the fact that most of the people caught on camera were stuffing hundreds and sometimes thousands of ballots into drop boxes. While it may be common practice for a family member or friend to drop a ballot off for someone they know, it's difficult to imagine there would be someone with a thousand friends who needed this assistance. Some of these mules were caught on camera going back to the same drop box multiple times on the same night. The argument against the geolocation data is extremely thin.

1. **Legitimate Multi-Ballot Drops:** *In many states, it is legal for people to drop off ballots on behalf of family members or others in their household. The fact that someone deposits more than one ballot does not necessarily indicate fraud.*

   When a mule makes over a dozen trips to the same drop box all while trying to conceal their identity, it's more than eyebrows that go up... It's usually their vote totals. I would encourage anyone who was led off the trail to take a hard look at the evidence. Watching these mules stuff hundreds of ballots into boxes on multiple occasions is jaw-dropping Again, once you see the evidence, this argument doesn't hold water.

2. **Lack of Concrete Evidence:** *Critics argue that the film relies heavily on circumstantial evidence and speculative conclusions without presenting conclusive proof of organized fraud. No court has accepted the evidence presented in* 2000 Mules *as proof of widespread fraud.* This statement is misleading considering the standing issues mentioned earlier. Juries have convicted murderers on an abundance of circumstantial evidence, in fact, the vast majority of trials are adjudicated on circumstantial evidence alone. So why would the naysayers want to lead you off this trail? Perhaps it's because they don't want you to know the truth. Our elections

should be sacred and protected at all costs. I think everyone involved in the process should want to make it as bulletproof as possible.

To the people who want to tout that there was no evidence of fraud in 2020, that is simply not true. From a multitude of states removing dead people or ineligible voters from the rolls who did indeed vote in 2020, to the abundance of mail-in votes found to be sent in error, the evidence is abundantly clear, and it makes a substantial case to overhaul our current election system in the United States. After all, if we've lost trust in the system itself, why do we even vote at all?

In the remainder of this chapter, I will outline three key reforms that can strengthen election integrity in the United States: requiring voter ID, returning to paper ballots, and designating Election Day as a national holiday, restricted to one day of voting. These measures not only safeguard the democratic process but also strike a balance between accessibility and security.

Voter ID: A Simple Safeguard

Requiring identification to vote is a basic measure that ensures only eligible citizens cast ballots. Critics argue that voter ID laws disenfranchise vulnerable populations, but the reality is that identification is required in nearly every aspect of life—from boarding a plane to opening a bank account, even getting into a nightclub. Implementing a voter ID law does not have to be exclusionary. Governments can offer free or low-cost IDs to individuals without one, making this requirement both inclusive and fair.

The argument against voter ID laws generally centers on concerns about accessibility and fairness in the voting process. Critics of voter ID laws argue that:

1. **Disenfranchisement:** Voter ID requirements may disproportionately affect certain groups, such as low-income individuals, minorities, the elderly, and people with disabilities. Objectors assert that these populations are less likely to have the required forms of identification and obtaining them may be costly or difficult.

2. **Unnecessary Burden:** Opponents argue that voter fraud, the main justification for voter ID laws, is extremely rare, so imposing ID requirements adds unnecessary hurdles to the democratic process without solving a significant problem.

3. **Discrimination:** Some believe that voter ID laws can perpetuate systemic inequalities by disproportionately affecting racial and ethnic minorities. Historical voter suppression tactics targeting minorities have fueled concerns that voter ID laws could have a similar effect.

4. **Administrative Burdens:** Implementing and enforcing voter ID laws may impose financial and administrative burdens on states, requiring additional resources for voter education, ID issuance, and training election officials.

These arguments don't make much logical sense, and if there was even a slight chance of voter fraud, one would think it would need to be addressed. For instance, we don't think twice about imposing ID restrictions in other areas in which it would be required. I would be curious to see an airline passenger try to make this argument at the ticket counter when buying a plane ticket, or a customer at a liquor store. Could the customer tell the clerk that they feel discriminated against because they can't afford the cost of an ID? In most counties across the United States, IDs are offered for free, and even people who do not have a driver's license or other state ID will obtain some form of ID to go about their daily business. I would wager that almost every single person who shows up at the polls on election day has an ID on them. While some may see ID requirements as an infringement on their Fifth Amendment rights, the overwhelming benefit it would have in eliminating nefarious activities would surely convince even the most staunch opponent.

The absence of ID requirements further opens the door to potential fraud and raises doubts about the accuracy of voter rolls. While cases of in-person voter fraud are rare, even the perception of vulnerability weakens confidence in the system. By mandating voter ID, we eliminate one major concern and provide a straightforward method for verifying that each vote cast is legitimate.

Countries around the world, including many in Europe, implement voter ID laws without facing the accusations of disenfranchisement or fraud that dominate the U.S. debate. A voter ID requirement simply adds a layer of accountability, ensuring that only eligible citizens participate in choosing their representatives.

Paper Ballots: The Gold Standard of Accountability

While digital voting machines have been touted for their efficiency, they come with significant risks. Machines can malfunction, be hacked, or miscalculate votes due to software errors. With recent cybersecurity threats targeting critical national infrastructure, it would be prudent to transition back to paper ballots, which provide a tangible, verifiable record of each vote.

Paper ballots are the gold standard when it comes to ensuring election integrity. They are immune to hacking and leave a clear audit trail that can be examined in the event of discrepancies. Additionally, the use of paper ballots reinforces transparency. When the voting process is physical and observable, it builds trust among voters and election monitors.

Hand-counting paper ballots—while more time-consuming—further enhances accountability. Election results may take longer to tabulate, but accuracy should never be sacrificed for speed. Some states and jurisdictions still conduct elections using paper ballots and manual counts, with minimal issues. Scaling this approach nationwide would restore confidence in the integrity of our elections.

Election Day: A National Holiday for a Single Day of Voting

Another critical reform would be to restore Election Day to a single day of voting, as opposed to the multi-week early voting process currently in place in many states. While early voting aims to improve voter turnout by offering flexibility, it introduces logistical and security complications. Different states have different rules about how early votes are handled and counted, leading to confusion and potential inconsistencies.

Furthermore, the extended voting period creates opportunities for political manipulation and chaos. Campaigns can use evolving events over weeks to sway voters who cast ballots early, before the full picture is clear. By limiting voting to one day, we level the playing field and ensure that all voters are making their decision based on the same information.

Making Election Day a national holiday would address concerns about accessibility. A holiday dedicated solely to voting ensures that every American, regardless of work or personal obligations, can participate. This reform would eliminate excuses about long lines or scheduling conflicts and increase voter turnout. Many countries, such as Germany and France, hold elections on weekends or make election days a national holiday to ensure maximum participation. There is no reason the United States cannot do the same.

Conclusion: Strengthening Our Democratic Foundation

The reforms proposed here—requiring voter ID, returning to paper ballots, and designating Election Day as a national holiday limited to one day of voting—are not about limiting access or turning back the clock. They are about restoring trust in our electoral system and ensuring that every vote counts fairly and securely.

In a democracy as large and complex as ours, no system will be perfect, but we must make election integrity our priority. Elections are the foundation of our republic, and if we fail to protect them, we risk undermining everything that makes America great.

7

REDUCING THE ADMINISTRATIVE STATE: RESTORING POWER TO THE PEOPLE

T HE GROWTH OF THE FEDERAL GOVERNMENT's administrative apparatus, often referred to as the "administrative state," represents
one of the most significant shifts in the structure and function
of American governance. The Founding Fathers envisioned
a limited federal government, designed to handle only the
essential functions, leaving most powers to the states and the
people. However, over the past century, the federal government
has grown exponentially, creating layers of bureaucracies and
agencies that seem increasingly distant from the electorate. As
these bureaucracies have expanded, so too has inefficiency,
waste, and detachment from democratic accountability.

President Donald J. Trump announced the Department of
Government Efficiency shortly after winning the 2024 Pres-
idential election. This department, commonly referred to as
DOGE, and originally headed up by Elon Musk and Vivek
Ramaswamy, is tasked with finding government inefficiency.
Elon Musk promised to cut $2 trillion from the Federal budget.
Musk and Ramaswamy also co-authored an op-ed in *The Wall
Street Journal* outlining their vision for the newly established
Department of Government Efficiency (DOGE). Their primary
objective is to streamline federal operations and significantly
reduce government spending. A key proposal involves mandat-
ing that all federal employees return to in-office work five days a
week, with the intention of encouraging voluntary resignations

from those unwilling to comply. This strategy aims to decrease the federal workforce and cut associated costs.

Additionally, DOGE advocates for the elimination of what they term "zombie" programs—federal initiatives that continue to receive funding despite lacking current congressional authorization. They argue that terminating these programs could save approximately $500 billion annually. Their approach also includes leveraging the Supreme Court to expand presidential powers, enabling more decisive action in rescinding regulations and restructuring federal agencies. This legal strategy is intended to facilitate the implementation of their efficiency measures. While their proposals have garnered support from those advocating for a leaner government, critics express concerns about potential disruptions to essential services and the loss of experienced federal employees. I believe the critics' arguments hold little weight given the dire fiscal situation the United States is facing. It's time to adopt these measures to help secure America's future! As of this writing, Ramaswamy has since left DOGE and announced his candidacy for Governor of Ohio. However, his influence has broad implications and has started the new agency off on the right track.

In this chapter, we will make the case that the federal government is bloated, wasteful, and could be cut by at least 75% without diminishing essential services. Reducing the administrative state would empower elected officials to regain control from unelected bureaucrats, restore democratic accountability, and streamline government services to better serve the American people.

The Growth of Bureaucracy: A Legacy of Expansion

Since the New Deal era of the 1930s, the federal government has increasingly taken on responsibilities that were once considered outside its scope. Agencies were created to regulate industries, manage social welfare programs, oversee environmental protections, and much more. The post-World War II era saw further expansion as the government sought to manage a complex modern economy and growing international commitments.

As of December 2024, the U.S. federal government employed approximately 3 million civilian workers. This number includes employees across various federal departments and agencies, excluding uniformed military personnel. These agencies exercise significant power, often writing and enforcing regulations that have the force of law—despite the fact that their leaders are not elected by the public.

Bureaucrats vs. Elected Officials: Who Holds the Power?

One of the central problems with the administrative state is that it shifts power away from elected officials and into the hands of unelected bureaucrats. Agencies like the Environmental Protection Agency (EPA), the Department of Education (ED), and the Food and Drug Administration (FDA) all have the power to issue rules that affect the lives of millions of Americans. Yet the heads of these agencies are appointed, not elected, and the career civil servants who work within them often remain in place regardless of the results of elections.

This situation creates a significant accountability gap. While Congress may pass broad legislation, the specifics of how that law is implemented are often left to the discretion of bureaucratic agencies. This means that much of the day-to-day governance of the country is in the hands of people who are not directly answerable to the voters. In contrast, elected officials— who are supposed to represent the will of the people—have ceded much of their authority to the bureaucratic apparatus.

The administrative state is also notoriously difficult to reform. Bureaucratic agencies often become entrenched, defending their budgets and expanding their mandates regardless of whether their programs are effective. The result is a bloated federal workforce that is expensive to maintain and often inefficient in its operations.

Waste and Inefficiency: A System in Need of Reform

The inefficiency of the administrative state is well-documented. Government waste—defined as unnecessary or inefficient spending—costs taxpayers billions of dollars annually. This waste occurs in numerous forms: duplicate programs, outdated technology, poor management, and excessive regulation. Reports from government watchdog organizations frequently highlight examples of redundancy, where multiple agencies perform similar or overlapping functions without coordination.

For example, the Government Accountability Office (GAO) identified multiple instances where several federal agencies are tasked with the same or very similar responsibilities, leading to confusion, duplication of effort, and unnecessary spending. This duplication extends to programs designed to address education, health care, energy, and infrastructure—areas where state or local governments could manage more efficiently with fewer federal mandates.

The administrative state also suffers from the inertia that plagues large organizations. Changing or reforming government programs is difficult, in part because bureaucrats are incentivized to preserve their jobs and the agencies they work for. Unlike the private sector, where inefficiency often leads to restructuring or downsizing, federal bureaucracy tends to perpetuate itself, with new positions and programs being added while outdated or redundant ones are rarely eliminated.

A 75% Reduction in the Federal Workforce: Why It's Feasible

Cutting the federal workforce by 75% might sound radical, but it is both feasible and necessary if we are to restore efficiency and accountability in government. Here's how:

1. **Reallocate Responsibilities to the States:** Many functions currently performed by federal agencies could be better managed at the state or local level. Education, housing, and environmental regulation are just a few areas where decentralization would allow for more tailored solutions that better reflect the needs of local populations. This would reduce the need for massive federal bureaucracies and empower states to innovate.

2. **Streamline Agencies and Cut Redundancy:** A significant proportion of the federal workforce is employed in agencies that have overlapping responsibilities. By consolidating these agencies and eliminating redundant functions, we could reduce the number of employees required to perform essential tasks. For example, merging similar programs across agencies or eliminating outdated offices could dramatically reduce the need for bureaucratic oversight.

3. **Leverage Technology:** Advances in technology have made many traditional bureaucratic functions obsolete. The private sector has embraced automation, artificial intelligence, and digital tools to streamline operations and reduce the need for large workforces. The federal government, by contrast, has been slow to adopt these innovations. By modernizing technology and automating routine tasks, the government could significantly reduce staffing levels while improving service delivery.

4. **Reform Regulatory Processes:** Much of the federal workforce is engaged in regulatory enforcement. However, many regulations are outdated or unnecessarily burdensome. By simplifying and reducing regulations, we can lessen the need for large numbers of enforcement agents and regulatory overseers. This would also benefit businesses and the economy, reducing compliance costs and encouraging innovation.

5. **Outsource Non-Essential Functions:** Many functions performed by the federal government could be outsourced to the private sector, where competition would encourage efficiency and cost-effectiveness. Non-essential services like IT management, human resources, and maintenance can often be performed better and more cheaply by private contractors.

Restoring Democratic Accountability

By reducing the size of the federal workforce and cutting back on the administrative state, we would also restore a crucial element of democratic accountability. When agencies are smaller and less powerful, more authority is returned to elected officials in Congress and the executive branch. This ensures that the people making decisions about how our country is governed are directly accountable to voters.

Currently, Congress passes massive pieces of legislation but often leaves the implementation of those laws to federal agencies. This delegation of authority has resulted in an out-of-control bureaucracy that often makes policy decisions without sufficient oversight. By reducing the number of bureaucrats and centralizing more decision-making with elected officials, we can ensure that government actions better reflect the will of the people.

Conclusion: A Leaner, More Accountable Government

The federal government has grown far beyond the scope envisioned by the Founding Fathers, resulting in a bloated, wasteful, and inefficient administrative state. By cutting the federal workforce by 75%, we can return power to the states, streamline government functions, and reduce wasteful spending. Most importantly, we can restore democratic accountability by ensuring that those who make decisions about our country's future are answerable to the voters, not to an entrenched bureaucratic class.

Reducing the size of the administrative state is not just a matter of efficiency; it is a matter of preserving the core principles of American democracy. A leaner, more focused government will serve the American people better and more efficiently, while also respecting the vision of limited government enshrined in the Constitution.

According to USA Today, the federal workforce grew by about 4.8% during Biden's term, increasing from 2.89 million in January 2021 to 3.02 million in January 2025. This number does not include the military or federal contractors, but it encompasses the civilian employees working in various federal departments, agencies, and sub-agencies.

Here's a breakdown of the major segments of the federal workforce:

1. **Executive Branch:**
   - Includes the vast majority of federal employees.
   - Agencies like the Department of Defense (civilian side), Department of Veterans Affairs, Department of Homeland Security, and the Department of Health and Human Services are some of the largest employers.

2. **Legislative Branch:**
   - This branch employs around 30,000 people.
   - It includes the staff of Congress, support agencies like the Government Accountability Office (GAO), the Library of Congress, and others.

3. **Judicial Branch:**
   - The judicial branch employs about 35,000 people.
   - This includes federal court employees, clerks, and administrative personnel.

4. **U.S. Postal Service:**
   - While technically a part of the federal government, the U.S. Postal Service operates independently and employs about **500,000 workers**. However, postal employees are generally considered separate from other civilian federal employees for most statistical purposes.

5. **Military Personnel:**

   - The active-duty military workforce consists of about **1.3 million** personnel, but they are not included in the over 3 million civilian figure.

6. **Contractors:**

   - The federal government also relies on contractors, though they are not considered direct federal employees. Estimates suggest there are millions of federal contractors working on government projects, though precise numbers vary.

If you factor in the total government presence, including military personnel and contractors, the broader workforce affiliated with the federal government becomes much larger. However, the **civilian workforce** (excluding military) remains the core of the federal administrative state, representing the 3 million figure typically cited.

As of 2025, the total U.S. civilian labor force is approximately **167 million people.** Given that the **federal workforce** consists of around **3 million civilian employees**, we can calculate the percentage of the federal workforce compared to the overall U.S. workforce.

Thus, the federal civilian workforce makes up about **1.8%** of the total U.S. labor force. This does not include military personnel or federal contractors, who would increase the size of the federal employment footprint if counted.

To calculate the broader footprint of the federal workforce, including military personnel and federal contractors, we need to combine estimates for these groups.

Here's a breakdown of the total workforce affiliated with the federal government:

1. **Federal Civilian Workforce:** Approximately **Over 3 million** employees.
2. **Active-Duty Military Personnel:** Approximately **1.3 million** service members.
3. **Federal Contractors:** Estimates vary widely, but it's commonly estimated that there are between **3 and 4 million** federal contractors working on government projects. For this calculation, we'll use a midpoint estimate of **3.5 million** contractors.

Calculating the Percentage of the U.S. Labor Force:

When including federal contractors and military personnel, the federal workforce footprint is approximately **4.67%** of the total U.S. labor force. This is a significant increase from the **1.8%** represented by the civilian federal workforce alone, reflecting the broader reliance on contractors and military personnel in the operation of the federal government.

To calculate the total percentage of U.S. employees who work for the government, we need to include federal, state, and local government employees, as well as those working for public schools and other government-funded institutions. Here's a breakdown of the various categories of government employment:

Breakdown of Government Employment:

Federal Civilian Employees: Approximately **3 million** (excluding military and contractors).

1. **Active-Duty Military Personnel:** Approximately **1.3 million.**
2. **State Government Employees:** Approximately **5.2 million.**

3. **Local Government Employees:** Approximately **14.2 million**, which includes:

   • **Public School Employees:** This category includes both state and local government employees who work in public education, including K-12 teachers, support staff, and higher education employees.

   • **Police, Firefighters, Public Works, etc.:** These are included in local government employment.

Total U.S. Government Workforce:

The total U.S. civilian labor force is approximately **167 million** people.

Approximately **14.24%** of the total U.S. workforce is employed by the government, including federal, state, and local government employees, as well as those working in public schools and other public institutions. This reflects the significant role that government plays in the employment landscape across the country.

The total payroll for federal civilian employees is a significant part of the federal budget. While precise figures can vary year to year, the Office of Personnel Management (OPM) and Congressional Budget Office (CBO) provide estimates that can help approximate the total cost.

Estimating the Combined Payroll for Federal Employees:

As of recent data:

⊙ The **average salary** for a federal civilian employee is approximately **$90,500** per year. This figure includes all federal employees, from lower-level staff to higher-paid professionals, and can fluctuate slightly depending on the agency and specific roles.

Conclusion

The estimated **combined payroll** for federal civilian employees is approximately **$190 billion** annually. This figure includes only the base salaries and does not account for additional benefits such as health insurance, retirement contributions, or bonuses, which would raise the overall cost of federal employment significantly.

Benefits often increase the total cost of employing federal workers by about 30-40%, meaning the overall compensation package could be closer to **$250-$270 billion** annually when benefits are included. This highlights the immense burden placed on taxpayers simply to sustain our bloated government. However, this is only one aspect; the true cost to taxpayers lies hidden in the regulations imposed by unelected bureaucrats on everyday citizens.

Code of Federal Regulations (CFR)

The U.S. federal government maintains an extensive array of regulations, codified in the **Code of Federal Regulations (CFR)**. The CFR is organized into 50 titles, each covering a broad area of federal regulation. As of recent estimates, the CFR comprises approximately **188,000 pages**. This vast compilation details the federal government's regulatory scope across various sectors, including environmental protection, labor, finance, and public health.

It's important to note that the CFR is continually updated to incorporate new regulations and amendments. The **Electronic Code of Federal Regulations (eCFR)** provides a regularly updated, unofficial version of the CFR, offering more current information on federal regulations. While the exact number of individual regulations is challenging to determine due to the complexity and varying lengths of regulatory provisions, the page count serves as a general indicator of the regulatory landscape's breadth.

During President Donald Trump's first term, the administration undertook significant deregulatory efforts. According to a 2018 fact sheet from the White House, the administration eliminated 22 regulations for every new one introduced in 2017, and 12 regulations for every new one in 2018.

These actions reportedly resulted in nearly $50 billion in regulatory cost savings, with projections of $220 billion in savings once major actions were fully implemented. However, it's important to note that these figures have been subject to scrutiny. Analyses by organizations like PolitiFact have indicated that the administration's claims may have been overstated, as they often counted deregulatory actions more broadly while being selective in counting new regulations. Additionally, many of the deregulatory actions faced legal challenges, and some were overturned in court.

In summary, while the Trump administration reported a significant reduction in regulations during its first term, the exact number and impact of these deregulatory actions are complex and have been the subject of debate.

Overregulation in the United States imposes significant financial burdens on businesses, which often translate into higher costs for consumers.

Financial Impact on Businesses:

Compliance Costs: In 2022, federal regulations cost the U.S. economy approximately $3.079 trillion, equating to 12% of the Gross Domestic Product (GDP).

The average U.S. firm incurred annual compliance costs of $277,000, representing 19% of payroll expenses.

- ⊚ **Disproportionate Burden on Small Businesses:** Small manufacturing firms with 20 employees faced compliance costs exceeding $1 million annually.

This disproportionate impact can hinder growth and innovation among smaller enterprises.

Effect on Consumer Costs:

Increased Prices: Regulatory compliance expenses are often passed on to consumers. A study found that a 10% increase in total regulations leads to a 0.687% rise in consumer prices.

This effect is particularly pronounced in heavily regulated sectors like energy and food, where consumers devote a significant portion of their budgets.

- ⊚ **Regressive Impact:** Higher prices due to regulatory costs disproportionately affect lower-income households, as they spend a larger share of their income on essential goods and services.

Conclusion

While regulations aim to protect public interests, excessive regulatory burdens can lead to substantial financial costs for businesses and higher prices for consumers. Balancing necessary regulations with economic efficiency is crucial to minimize adverse economic impacts. The number of regulations varies significantly across U.S. states. According to the Mercatus Center's 2024 analysis, the average state has approximately **136,262 regulations**. This figure reflects the diverse regulatory environments tailored to each state's unique economic, social, and political contexts.

For instance, California is noted for having the most extensive regulatory framework among the states, while states like South Carolina and Michigan are recognized for having fewer regulations. These variations underscore the importance of understanding state-specific regulatory landscapes, especially for businesses and individuals operating across multiple jurisdictions.

Here are some examples of federal regulations that have been criticized as excessive, overly complex, or absurd, often cited in debates about the scope of government oversight:

1. Restrictions on "Spilled Milk"
The Environmental Protection Agency (EPA) once regulated milk spills under the same rules as oil spills, requiring dairy farmers to prepare "emergency management plans" for spilled milk. The rationale was that milk contains animal fat, which is classified as oil. This regulation was eventually rolled back after public outcry.

2. Regulating the Size of Holes in Swiss Cheese
The federal government enforces standards on the size of holes in Swiss cheese. According to USDA rules, the holes must not be too big or too small, as they could impact consumer perception and slicing efficiency.

3. Declaring Pizza as a Vegetable

In 2011, Congress declared that a slice of pizza with a specific amount of tomato paste could qualify as a vegetable in school lunch programs. Critics saw this as a result of lobbying rather than science or nutrition.

4. Bathroom Signs for Service Animals

The Americans with Disabilities Act (ADA) mandates that service animals must be accommodated in public restrooms, and in some cases, signs indicating this must be posted. Critics argue this is unnecessary for most situations and facilities.

5. Regulations on Pillow Tags

Federal law requires pillows to have tags stating their materials and warning consumers not to remove the tag "under penalty of law." While this is meant to inform consumers, the language has often been misunderstood to mean individuals cannot remove the tags, sparking unnecessary confusion. The tags exist to protect consumers. Historically, some manufacturers used recycled or even unsanitary materials in mattresses without disclosing it. To prevent deception, U.S. laws required that mattresses be labeled with contents, similar to food ingredient labels. If you are the end user, feel free to rip those tags off, nobody is filing charges!

6. The Volume of Water in Toilets

The Energy Policy Act of 1992 set maximum water usage for toilets at 1.6 gallons per flush, leading to complaints about inefficiency and the need for multiple flushes. This prompted debates about whether the federal government should regulate personal bathroom use.

7. Limits on Balloons for Children
The Consumer Product Safety Commission (CPSC) has regulations limiting the types of balloons that can be sold for children due to choking hazards. While safety is a concern, critics argue that such rules can be overly restrictive and burdensome.

8. Bans on Catching Migratory Birds by Accident
Under the Migratory Bird Treaty Act, it is illegal to "take" migratory birds without a permit, even if the action is accidental (e.g., wind turbines or oil spills). Critics say this regulation imposes significant costs and legal risks on industries without clear environmental benefits.

9. Control Over Light Bulbs
Federal regulations phased out incandescent light bulbs in favor of energy-efficient alternatives, which some critics viewed as an unnecessary intrusion into consumer choice.

10. Children's Books and Lead Testing
A law intended to reduce lead in children's toys required books published before 1985 to be tested for lead, leading to concerns that libraries might have to discard old books. This requirement was later clarified (there was no lead involved in the bookmaking process) but caused confusion and alarm when first introduced.

11. Licensing for Flower Arrangers
Some states, under federal occupational licensing frameworks, have regulated professions such as flower arranging. Critics argue that these regulations create unnecessary barriers to entry in small, low-risk industries.

12. The "Eel Ladder"

A federal regulation requires the construction of "eel ladders" at hydroelectric dams to help eels migrate upstream. While the intention is environmental conservation, critics highlight the unusual specificity and cost of such rules.

Conclusion

While many regulations serve important purposes, these examples illustrate how some rules can appear unnecessary, overly specific, or burdensome. Addressing regulatory inefficiency while preserving essential protections is a key focus in ongoing debates about reform.

I've often argued—both in conversations and on my show—that the public would be better served if newly elected members of Congress simply went to work and did absolutely nothing. One of the biggest issues we face, which ties directly into the term limits debate, is that Congress is perpetually in campaign mode. Even a well-intentioned conservative can quickly abandon their principles upon taking the oath of office. Why? Because in the short, two-year House term, members must start campaigning almost immediately to secure their next term. Re-election depends on "bringing home the bacon" to their district—securing pet projects, pork-barrel spending, and other forms of government largesse. Without those earmarks, they won't get their names on bridges or schools back home. This endless cycle fuels runaway spending, balloons the national debt, and threatens the financial future of our children and grandchildren. It's unsustainable, and the numbers make that clear.

Consider the eagerness of Congress to take action—often under the banner of "doing something"—even when their decisions place undue burdens on the rest of us. The number of bills introduced by individual members of the U.S. Congress varies significantly based on factors such as chamber (House or Senate), party affiliation, seniority, and personal legislative priorities. Historically, the average number of bills introduced per member has fluctuated. According to the Brookings Institution, it looks like this:

- ⊚ **Mid-20th Century:** During the 80th Congress (1947-1948), the average was approximately 17.5 bills per member.
- ⊚ **Late 20th Century:** In the 95th Congress (1977-1978), the average increased to about 38 bills per member.
- ⊚ **Early 21st Century:** By the 115th Congress (2017-2018), the average had decreased to around 20 bills per member.

Keep in mind that there are 435 members in the House of Representatives and 50 U.S. Senators. If we were to calculate the number of bills for the 115th Congress, we get 535 times 20, which is a staggering 10,700 proposed bills over a two-year term. These averages reflect broader legislative trends and changes in congressional practices over time. It's important to note that while the number of bills introduced provides some insight into legislative activity, it doesn't necessarily correlate with the number of bills passed or the overall effectiveness of a legislator.

During the 115th United States Congress (2017–2018), a total of **758 bills** were passed by both the House of Representatives and the Senate. Of these, **443 bills** were signed into law by the President. That's 443 bills that most likely increased spending and forced more regulations on the citizens of this country. It's important to note that the volume of legislation has increased over time. In recent years, Congress has passed an average of approximately 344 new laws per session, each averaging 18 pages in length. This marks a significant increase from the 1950s, when bills averaged about two pages. What do you think is buried in those additional 16 pages?

8

MERIT VS. DEI

THE DEBATE BETWEEN MERIT-BASED SYSTEMS AND Diversity, Equity, and Inclusion (DEI) initiatives is one of the most polarizing in modern policy and organizational discussions. Proponents of merit argue that it rewards hard work, talent, and achievement, fostering an environment where the best ideas and the most capable individuals rise to the top. They claim that prioritizing merit ensures efficiency, innovation, and excellence, as decisions are based on measurable accomplishments rather than subjective criteria. In this view, a meritocratic system is the fairest and most effective way to allocate resources, opportunities, and recognition, maintaining a level playing field.

On the other hand, advocates for DEI emphasize the importance of addressing systemic inequalities that have historically marginalized certain groups. They argue that focusing solely on merit often overlooks barriers that prevent equal access to opportunities, such as socioeconomic disparities, implicit bias, and structural discrimination. DEI initiatives seek to level the playing field by creating policies that promote representation, inclusivity, and equitable outcomes. Proponents believe that a more diverse and inclusive environment enriches organizations, bringing a broader range of perspectives, fostering creativity, and reflecting the makeup of the society it serves.

Critics of meritocracy highlight its potential blind spots, such as perpetuating privilege. They argue that individuals often achieve success not solely through effort or ability but also through inherited advantages, such as access to quality education or professional networks. Conversely, opponents of DEI initiatives often express concern that these programs may sacrifice excellence or fairness by prioritizing identity over capability. They worry that such policies can lead to tokenism, resentment, and unintended divisions, ultimately undermining the goals of unity and equality.

I will argue that these DEI initiatives have contributed to America's decline by undermining the principles of meritocracy and fostering division rather than unity. I contend that prioritizing identity over qualifications has eroded standards in education, employment, and governance, leading to inefficiency and mediocrity. By emphasizing group identity, DEI is seen as creating a culture of entitlement and victimhood, where individuals are rewarded for their demographic characteristics rather than their achievements. This shift, some argue, has stifled innovation, weakened institutions, and fueled resentment among those who feel excluded or unfairly disadvantaged by these policies. In this view, DEI has moved the country away from a shared sense of excellence and common purpose, replacing it with polarization and declining trust in foundational systems.

At the conclusion of 2024 and leading into 2025, several prominent organizations have scaled back or dismantled their Diversity, Equity, and Inclusion (DEI) departments. Notable examples include:

- **Boeing:** The aerospace giant disbanded its global DEI department, integrating its functions into broader human resources teams.
- **Brown-Forman Corp.:** The maker of Jack Daniel's whiskey ceased its DEI initiatives following social media pressure and boycott threats.

- ⊚ **Harley-Davidson:** The motorcycle manufacturer ended its DEI programs, citing a need to focus on core business objectives.
- ⊚ **Toyota:** The automaker announced a refocus of its DEI programs and ceased sponsorship of LGBTQ+ events.
- ⊚ **Tractor Supply Co.:** The retailer eliminated DEI roles and withdrew from various DEI-related activities.

This trend reflects a broader reassessment of DEI initiatives across corporate America, influenced by legal challenges, political opposition, and debates over the effectiveness of such programs.

I can make a strong case against policies that discriminate under the guise of fairness. I am a white individual who would never list myself as a minority on any application, yet in today's world, I often feel like one. I grew up in a middle-class household, one of two children raised by divorced parents. At 15, I moved out, spending years on the streets. I bounced between friends' homes before I started living in my car at age 17. Despite these challenges, I worked hard to turn my life around. At 17, I started my first company, and at 26, I went to college. By 29, I had graduated from the police academy, only to face unexpected roadblocks caused by DEI initiatives in government hiring.

Despite scoring high on civil service exams, my results were viewed differently because I was not considered a minority. Preference was given to others based solely on race or gender, even if they scored lower. This systemic bias—disguised as diversity—is, in reality, a form of institutionalized racism. The rationale was that, as a white person, I had more opportunities and therefore needed to be penalized. Yet, no one considered the fact that I was homeless and had clawed my way back from nothing. The only factors that mattered were race and gender—not merit or individual circumstances.

This unfair treatment extended beyond civil service. When I applied for government contracts with my business, I discovered preferences for Women-Owned Business Enterprises (WBEs) and Minority-Owned Business Enterprises (MBEs). These entities received a 5% bidding advantage. For example, if I bid $99,000 for a contract and a WBE or MBE bid $104,000, they would win, as their bid would be adjusted to $98,800 for evaluation purposes—even though the government would pay the full $104,000. This meant I lost contracts to companies that cost more, all because of policies that prioritized gender and race over qualifications and value.

Such policies not only disregard fairness but undermine the idea of hiring or contracting based on merit. They ignore individual struggles and achievements, like my journey from homelessness to entrepreneurship, in favor of blanket assumptions based on identity. That doesn't reflect a just system, nor does it ensure the best and brightest are selected for opportunities. It's a disservice to everyone involved. I highlight this to demonstrate that my perspective is not theoretical. I have witnessed these policies in action, both their successes and failures, across the nation. Our current system increasingly selects winners and losers based on political ideologies that often diverge from the realities on the ground.

On June 29, 2023, the U.S. Supreme Court ruled that race-based affirmative action in college admissions is unconstitutional, effectively ending such practices in higher education. The Court's decision addressed cases involving Harvard University and the University of North Carolina, concluding that their admissions programs violated the Equal Protection Clause of the Fourteenth Amendment. Chief Justice John Roberts, writing for the majority, stated that while universities can consider an applicant's discussion of how race has affected their life, race itself cannot be a factor in admissions decisions. This ruling overturned previous precedents, including Grutter v. Bollinger (2003) and Regents of the University of California v. Bakke (1978), which had permitted limited consideration of race in admissions to promote diversity.

The decision has prompted universities to reevaluate their admissions policies to comply with the new legal framework. Some institutions are exploring alternative methods to achieve diverse student bodies without considering race directly. For example, the University of Richmond is assessing its first admission class following the affirmative action ban, emphasizing the importance of evaluating students on their merits. Additionally, California has enacted legislation banning legacy admissions in private colleges, aiming to create a more equitable admissions process. This move reflects a broader trend of reassessing traditional admissions practices in light of the Supreme Court's ruling.

The ruling has also influenced corporate diversity initiatives. Companies are facing new challenges in promoting diversity, equity, and inclusion (DEI) programs, with some adjusting their criteria to avoid explicit racial preferences and mitigate legal risks. The Supreme Court's decision to abolish affirmative action in college admissions marks a significant shift in higher education and beyond, prompting institutions and organizations to seek new approaches to fostering diversity within the constraints of the law.

DEI in the Military

Until recently, Diversity, Equity, and Inclusion were integral components of the U.S. military's efforts to build a force that reflects the nation's diversity and upholds principles of fairness and respect. The Department of Defense (DoD) implemented various initiatives to promote DEI across all branches of the armed forces. The Office for Diversity, Equity, and Inclusion (ODEI) within the DoD developed and executed policies affecting military personnel and civilian employees. This office focused on attracting, recruiting, developing, and retaining a highly skilled and diverse workforce to meet mission requirements. However, this narrative is illogical. Personally, I want the best and brightest. If you're standing with me in a firefight, I need to trust that your qualifications are solid and well-earned. It wouldn't sit well with me knowing you were placed there just to satisfy a bureaucratic quota.

Strategic Plans and Policies

In September 2022, the DoD released its Diversity, Equity, Inclusion, and Accessibility (DEIA) Strategic Plan for Fiscal Years 2022-2023. This plan outlined a path for advancing DEIA across the Department, supporting efforts to build a workforce capable of maintaining readiness to deter war and ensure national security. How these words ended up in the same sentence is beyond me. It seems like U.S. taxpayers have poured a lot of money into sidestepping logic and crafting language designed to make these ideas more acceptable to the public. What I need is a military that's well-trained and fully prepared to defend our nation. I had no idea we were allocating resources to rebranding policies just to ease public discomfort.

Training and Education

The Defense Equal Opportunity Management Institute (DEOMI) provided training and research in areas such as equal opportunity, intercultural communication, and diversity. Established in 1971, DEOMI offered courses and conducted research to support the readiness of civilian and military personnel working with the American armed forces.

Challenges and Criticisms

Despite these efforts, DEI initiatives in the military faced challenges and criticisms. Some studies suggest that DEI efforts may have been ineffective and ran counter to the military ethos, arguing that such programs distract from essential military objectives and undermine team cohesion.

Legislative Actions and Future

In October 2023, Congress considered significant rollbacks of the military's DEI programs as part of the Fiscal Year 2024 Defense Department appropriations bill. This move reflected ongoing debates about the role and impact of DEI initiatives within the armed forces. This raised a larger question: how many members of our armed forces are truly the best and brightest? Had we lowered our standards to the point where the quality of our military was at risk?

President Trump appointed Pete Hegseth as Secretary of Defense during his second administration, and I believe this was an excellent choice. Pete is a two-time Bronze Star recipient with over 20 years of military service, including combat experience. His perspectives on the military have been consistently public and well-documented. Beyond his distinguished service, Pete has been a prominent Fox News personality for over a decade and has authored numerous books on military topics. His views are transparent and thoroughly vetted. Now that Pete Hegseth has been confirmed, I know he will bring much-needed reform to our armed forces, ensuring we maintain the world's most capable fighting force—a force focused on its core mission, and not distracted by divisive DEI narratives. At the time of this writing, the Trump administration has been advancing at an incredible pace. Even those of us closely following politics find it challenging to keep up. Significant policy changes have already been implemented under Pete Hegseth and through executive orders signed by Donald Trump. These reforms, which I fully support, will help steer the country back on track and ensure we maintain the strongest and most capable fighting force in the world.

How Do We Move Forward?

In a nation as diverse and vibrant as the United States, the best way to move forward is by recognizing what unites us all: our shared humanity. For decades, policies rooted in Diversity, Equity, and Inclusion (DEI) have sought to address disparities and promote fairness. While some may have thought this was well-intentioned, these policies have often fallen short, fostering division rather than unity and failing to achieve their desired outcomes. It's time to move beyond the antiquated frameworks of DEI and adopt a perspective that treats every individual equally—no labels, no quotas, just humans.

Historical Context and Purpose of DEI

DEI policies emerged during a critical period in American history when overt discrimination and systemic inequality were rampant. These policies aimed to rectify historical injustices and provide opportunities to marginalized groups. Early successes included breaking barriers in employment, education, and public life. However, as time progressed, the social and economic landscape evolved. America today is more diverse than ever, with countless avenues of opportunity available to all. Yet, DEI policies have not adapted to these changes. Instead, they continue to operate on outdated assumptions that categorize individuals by race, gender, or ethnicity rather than valuing them for their unique capabilities and contributions.

Problems with DEI in Practice

While the goals of DEI may sound noble, their application often produces unintended and counterproductive outcomes. For example:

- **Tokenism Over Inclusion:** DEI policies frequently emphasize representation over merit, leading to tokenism that undermines genuine inclusion. Individuals hired or promoted under these systems may feel devalued, while their colleagues question the fairness of the process.
- **Division and Resentment:** Categorizing people into groups based on identity fosters an "us vs. them" mentality. Instead of bridging divides, DEI often exacerbates them, creating resentment among those who feel overlooked or unfairly treated.
- **Overlooking Merit and Competence:** DEI initiatives sometimes prioritize identity over qualifications, diluting the importance of competence. This not only hampers organizational performance but also demoralizes individuals who excel based on their abilities.

- **Legal and Practical Challenges:** DEI mandates can lead to lawsuits and compliance burdens that drain resources from organizations, further illustrating their inefficiency.

Why Equality Is Better Than Equity

The key distinction between equality and equity lies at the heart of this debate. Equality ensures that everyone has the same opportunities to succeed, while equity attempts to guarantee equal outcomes. The latter approach is inherently flawed because it disregards individual effort, talent, and ambition.

By focusing on equality:

- Individuals are judged on their merits, not their identity.
- Organizations can foster environments where innovation thrives because the best ideas rise to the top.
- Society as a whole becomes more cohesive, as people rally around shared values rather than divisive labels.

Proposed Alternatives to DEI Policies

Replacing DEI doesn't mean abandoning the pursuit of fairness—it means pursuing fairness through better means. Here are some alternatives:

- **Blind Recruitment Processes:** Remove names, genders, and other identifying markers from resumes to focus purely on qualifications and achievements.
- **Universal Education and Training:** Invest in programs that elevate all individuals, particularly those from disadvantaged socioeconomic backgrounds, regardless of race or gender.

- ◉ **Merit-Based Opportunities:** Prioritize skills, talent, and hard work over superficial characteristics. Reward individuals who demonstrate excellence and innovation.
- ◉ **Address Socioeconomic Barriers:** Shift the focus from identity-based programs to initiatives that target poverty, lack of access to education, and other systemic barriers that affect people across all demographics.

These solutions not only uphold fairness but also align with the American ideal that hard work and determination should determine success.

A Vision for the Future

Imagine an America where individuals are seen not as representatives of groups but as unique contributors to a greater whole. In this future, opportunities are abundant for those who seek them, and merit is the sole determinant of success. People no longer feel pressured to fit into predefined categories or compete against arbitrary quotas. Instead, they thrive in an environment that values innovation, collaboration, and respect for individual differences.

Such a society is not a utopian dream—it is a practical and attainable goal. By treating every individual as a human being with inherent dignity and value, we can create a nation that truly reflects the ideals of liberty and justice for all.

Conclusion

Diversity, Equity, and Inclusion policies may have had their moment in history, but their time has passed. They are now outdated frameworks that often do more harm than good. It is time to replace them with policies and practices that prioritize equality, merit, and individual dignity. By moving beyond the divisive constructs of DEI, we can embrace our shared humanity and build a stronger, more united America. Let us remember that progress is not about dividing people into categories. It is about bringing them together as equals, united in the common pursuit of a better future.

To dismantle Diversity, Equity, and Inclusion (DEI) policies while ensuring fairness for all individuals, the United States must pivot toward a system rooted in merit and universal standards. The focus should be on creating opportunities for individuals to excel based on their skills, talents, and efforts, rather than categorizing them by race, gender, or ethnicity. By embracing a merit-based approach, society can move beyond the divisive frameworks that have come to define DEI and instead foster unity and shared purpose.

This shift must be accompanied by cultural and organizational change. Institutions should promote shared values such as respect, collaboration, and excellence, moving away from divisive DEI training programs that often foster resentment and resistance. Instead, workshops on unbiased decision-making and merit-based evaluations can guide leaders in creating environments where fairness and competence are paramount. Combined with transparency in outcomes and strong legal protections against discrimination, this approach can ensure a society where everyone is valued for their contributions, and success is determined by merit alone.

By adopting these measures, the U.S. can build a more unified and inclusive society that values individuals for their abilities rather than their identities. This shift away from DEI policies toward a merit-based framework not only upholds fairness but also aligns with the principles of equality and opportunity that underpin the American dream.

If we genuinely aspire to be a melting pot that reflects our diversity and progress, we must unite under a single banner— the American flag. The ongoing self-segregation, compounded by government and DEI policies, has only deepened the divides within our nation. To truly become one nation, under God, with liberty and justice for all, we must abandon the practice of choosing winners and losers. This approach is not only logical but essential to securing America's future.

9

FREEDOM OF SPEECH

You MAY WONDER WHY I FELT I had to include a chapter on freedom of speech. I mean, after all, that's something that *is* guaranteed under the Constitution. Well, as Bill Clinton once famously said, "It depends on what your meaning of the word 'is' is." From my experience of having my books censored or shadow-banned, my interviews removed from social media, and being blocked from advertising my products, I've found freedom of speech often depends on who is speaking, who is interpreting the message, and who is responsible for protecting free speech. It also hinges on the financial resources available to expose and address these issues.

The U.S. Constitution guarantees freedom of speech through the First Amendment, which states:

> *"Congress shall make no law respecting an establishment of religion, or prohibiting the free exercise thereof; or abridging the freedom of speech, or of the press; or the right of the people peaceably to assemble, and to petition the Government for a redress of grievances."*

Key Points About Freedom of Speech in the Constitution:

1. **Scope and Protection:**
   - The First Amendment protects individuals from government interference with their speech. This means that Congress, and by extension state and local governments (via the incorporation doctrine under the 14th Amendment), cannot impose laws that suppress free expression.
   - It does not provide absolute protection. Certain types of speech, such as incitement to violence or defamation, may be regulated.

2. **Limitations:** While broad, freedom of speech is not unlimited. The U.S. Supreme Court has defined specific exceptions:
   - **Incitement of Violence:** Speech that incites imminent lawless action (e.g., riots) can be restricted (Brandenburg v. Ohio, 1969).
   - **Obscenity:** Obscene material that lacks serious literary, artistic, political, or scientific value is not protected (Miller v. California, 1973).
   - **Defamation:** False statements that harm a person's reputation can be restricted if made with actual malice or negligence.
   - **Threats:** True threats, which are serious expressions of intent to commit violence, are not protected.
   - **Commercial Speech:** While protected, it is subject to greater regulation to prevent fraud or harm.

2. **Content-Neutrality:**
   - The government generally cannot regulate speech based on its content. Laws restricting speech must pass strict scrutiny, meaning they must serve a compelling governmental interest and be narrowly tailored.

3. **Public vs. Private Regulation:**
   - The First Amendment only restricts government actions. It does not apply to private entities, such as businesses or social media platforms, which are free to set their own rules regarding speech.

4. **Symbolic Speech:**
   - The Supreme Court has ruled that nonverbal actions intended to convey a message, such as flag burning (Texas v. Johnson, 1989), are protected under the First Amendment.

Implications

The First Amendment is a cornerstone of American democracy, ensuring that individuals can express opinions, debate, and criticize the government without fear of retaliation. However, its interpretation evolves as courts address new challenges in areas like digital communication and misinformation.

Section 230 refers to a provision in the United States' **Communications Decency Act (CDA)** of 1996, codified at **47 U.S.C. § 230**. It is a foundational law for the modern internet, providing critical protections for online platforms and social media companies. Here's an explanation of what it is and how it works:

What is Section 230?

Section 230 states:

1. **Interactive computer services (like social media platforms)** are not treated as the publisher or speaker of information provided by third-party users. This means that platforms like Facebook, Twitter, YouTube, or forums are not held legally responsible for most of the content posted by their users.
2. Platforms are granted **broad immunity** from liability for user-generated content, with some exceptions, such as content related to federal criminal activity or intellectual property violations.
3. It allows platforms to moderate content in **good faith** without losing this protection, meaning they can remove or restrict material they consider obscene, lewd, violent, or otherwise objectionable, even if it is constitutionally protected speech.

How Does It Protect Social Media Companies?

1. **Immunity from Liability for User-Generated Content:** Social media platforms are shielded from lawsuits over harmful or illegal content posted by users, such as defamatory comments or misinformation. Without this immunity, platforms could face overwhelming litigation and might severely restrict user interactions.
2. **Freedom to Moderate Content:** Section 230 enables platforms to remove or moderate content they find objectionable without being considered publishers. This

"good faith" clause gives platforms flexibility to curate
and enforce community guidelines.

3. **Encourages Innovation:** By reducing the legal risks
associated with user-generated content, Section 230
fosters the growth of new internet platforms. Without
it, companies might be reluctant to allow users to post
freely, which could stifle the interactive nature of online
communities.

Criticisms of Section 230

- **Too Much Power for Platforms:** Critics argue it gives
tech companies the power to act as gatekeepers of information, censoring certain viewpoints.
- **Shielding Harmful Activity:** Others claim that immunity
allows platforms to avoid responsibility for harmful content, like misinformation, hate speech, or exploitation.
- **Calls for Reform:** There have been bipartisan calls to
amend Section 230, with proposals ranging from increasing transparency about moderation policies to removing immunity for specific types of harmful content.

In short, Section 230 has been pivotal in shaping the internet
as we know it, granting platforms the freedom to host diverse
content while limiting their liability. However, the debate over
its scope and implications continues to evolve.

In early 2024, the House Judiciary Committee, led by Chair-
man Jim Jordan, released internal communications between the
Biden administration and Amazon. These documents suggest
that the White House exerted pressure on Amazon to limit

the visibility of books expressing skepticism about COVID-19 vaccines.

Key Findings:

- ⊚ **White House Concerns:** In March 2021, Andrew Slavitt, then a senior adviser for COVID-19 response, emailed Amazon officials expressing concern over search results for "vaccines" that surfaced content the administration deemed problematic. He questioned, "Who can we talk to about the high levels of propaganda and misinformation and disinformation of [sic] Amazon?"
- ⊚ **Amazon's Initial Response:** Initially, Amazon decided against manual intervention to alter search results, citing concerns about visibility and potential backlash from media outlets. Internal communications indicated a reluctance to make changes that could attract negative attention.
- ⊚ **Subsequent Actions:** Despite initial hesitations, Amazon met with White House officials on March 9, 2021. On the same day, Amazon implemented a "Do Not Promote" policy for books questioning vaccine efficacy and considered additional measures to reduce the visibility of such titles.

These revelations have sparked debates about government influence over private companies and the balance between combating misinformation and upholding free speech. Critics argue that such actions may constitute undue censorship, while proponents contend they were necessary to protect public health during the pandemic.

The exact number of books affected by Amazon's actions in response to the Biden administration's concerns about COVID-19 vaccine misinformation is not definitively known. However, reports indicate that the administration pressured Amazon to censor 43 vaccine-critical books, including titles that were published before the COVID-19 pandemic.

These actions covered a diverse array of works, ranging from children's picture books to critical analyses of the pharmaceutical industry. Sadly, two of those books were mine! My first book, *Fauci's Fiction*—which isn't about Anthony Fauci but rather the data my own company collected during the COVID-19 pandemic—faced heavy censorship. Amazon even barred me from promoting it. Despite this, the book has been widely praised and recognized as one of the most valuable sources of information on COVID-19, yet it was censored and shadow-banned.

My second book, *Vaccine Fiction*, encountered significantly less censorship upon its release in late 2024, but by then, the damage had already been done. Even now, when I post about it on certain social media platforms, the algorithm suppresses visibility, limiting its reach to only a small audience. The Federal Government's role in orchestrating these actions has long been embedded in the algorithms of social media giants, and reversing this course will require direct intervention by these companies.

Recently, I hosted a guest on *2 Mikes Live* on Rumble. We also share our shows on platforms like YouTube and X. My guest was Brianne Dressen, author of *Worth a Shot: The Brianne Dressen Story*. Her book details her experience as a participant in a vaccine trial that resulted in an injury.

Since I only had 15 minutes with her on our evening show, I invited her to appear on my morning show, *The Mike Schwartz*

Show, where we could have a full hour to discuss her case in depth. Her vaccine injury was officially documented and confirmed by the National Institutes of Health—meaning our own government acknowledged that her injury was caused by the trial.

The day after our interview aired, despite the discussion being factual and not particularly controversial, YouTube emailed me stating that my account had been permanently banned for "medical misinformation." They claimed their decision was based on a combination of text analysis and human review. However, whoever these "human reviewers" are, they clearly have biases.

This situation highlights the cost of free speech on social media platforms. Those who speak out and share the truth risk being deplatformed. For content creators who rely on YouTube for their livelihood, there's a clear, chilling effect—many now avoid mentioning words like "Covid" or anything related to vaccines altogether.

If we want to save America, protecting free speech must be our top priority. It's not just about having it written in the Constitution, where only those with the time and money can fight their way to the Supreme Court for justice. The reality is that most people can't afford to defend their speech. It's time for an open discussion on this issue and to hold social media companies accountable, as they now serve as the primary platforms for public discourse in our country.

10

DIGITAL CURRENCY AND GOVERNMENT CONTROL

DIGITAL CURRENCY, A RELATIVELY MODERN FINANCIAL innovation, has become a topic of heated debate. Proponents argue it heralds a new era of efficiency and inclusivity, while critics highlight its risks, including potential government overreach and erosion of financial privacy. As the U.S. debates whether to adopt a Central Bank Digital Currency (CBDC), it is crucial to examine the history, current implementations, and potential consequences. This chapter argues against the widespread adoption of digital currency, especially government-issued forms, by highlighting its potential misuse as a tool for social and financial control.

The Origins of Digital Currency

The concept of digital currency predates the popularization of cryptocurrencies. In the 1990s, early forms of electronic money like DigiCash attempted to revolutionize online payments. However, these initiatives faced challenges, such as a lack of infrastructure and regulatory scrutiny.

Bitcoin, introduced in 2009 by the pseudonymous Satoshi Nakamoto, marked a turning point. It was designed as a decentralized digital currency, free from government control. Bitcoin's success inspired thousands of other cryptocurrencies, leading to the creation of a $3 trillion industry by 2021. These currencies promised faster transactions, reduced fees, and financial inclusion for the unbanked.

In response, governments worldwide began exploring their own versions of digital currencies—Central Bank Digital Currencies (CBDCs). Unlike cryptocurrencies, CBDCs are centralized and fully controlled by the issuing government.

Digital Currency in Practice: Global Case Studies
Countries like China, Sweden, and the Bahamas have already implemented CBDCs to varying degrees.

1. **China's Digital Yuan**
   China's Digital Yuan is currently one of the most advanced CBDC projects. It allows the government to track transactions in real time and implement policies such as negative interest rates. Critics argue that it gives the Chinese Communist Party unprecedented surveillance powers, allowing them to punish dissenters by restricting access to funds.
2. **Sweden's e-Krona**
   Sweden's e-Krona project aims to complement cash as the nation moves toward becoming a cashless society. While it promises convenience, concerns have arisen about the exclusion of people who lack digital literacy or access to technology.
3. **Bahamas' Sand Dollar**
   The Bahamas introduced the Sand Dollar to address financial inclusion in its archipelago. While it has succeeded in reaching remote communities, its limited adoption highlights the challenges of implementing digital currencies at scale.

The Case Against Digital Currency

1. Erosion of Financial Privacy

Digital currencies, particularly CBDCs, allow governments to monitor every transaction. Unlike cash, which offers anonymity, digital currencies can create a permanent, traceable record of every payment. In a society that values freedom, such surveillance undermines the privacy of individuals and businesses.

For example, a government could use transaction data to identify spending patterns, political affiliations, or even ideological beliefs. This level of surveillance poses a grave threat to civil liberties.

2. Enabling Government Overreach

A CBDC could give governments the power to restrict or condition how citizens spend their money. For instance:

- Funds could be programmed to expire after a certain period, forcing people to spend rather than save.
- Spending could be restricted to certain categories, such as barring purchases of certain goods or services deemed "undesirable."
- Governments could freeze or seize accounts with a few keystrokes, bypassing due process.

Such tools could be used to enforce compliance with controversial policies or punish dissent, transforming financial systems into mechanisms of control.

3. Increased Risk of Cybersecurity Threats

A centralized digital currency system creates a single point of failure. If hackers breach a CBDC's infrastructure, they could disrupt the entire economy. The stakes are much higher than in traditional banking systems because a CBDC would consolidate financial activity into one digital framework.

Historical examples, such as the 2016 hack of Bangladesh's central bank or the frequent attacks on cryptocurrency exchanges, underscore the risks of digital financial systems.

4. Economic Disruption and Financial Exclusion

Transitioning to a digital currency could destabilize existing financial systems. Commercial banks, which rely on customer deposits to fund loans, could see their roles diminished as individuals shift funds to CBDC accounts. This could lead to reduced credit availability and increased economic inequality.

Additionally, digital currency adoption risks excluding vulnerable populations, such as the elderly, low-income individuals, and rural communities, who may lack access to the necessary technology or internet connectivity.

5. The Loss of Cash and Its Implications

Cash provides a backup during natural disasters, cyberattacks, or infrastructure failures. Eliminating cash in favor of digital currency creates a single point of dependency on technology. If systems fail, society could face chaos, with no viable alternative for transactions.

Furthermore, cash serves as a safeguard for financial autonomy. It allows individuals to engage in private transactions, whether tipping a service worker or donating anonymously to a cause. A cashless society risks losing this essential flexibility.

Lessons from History: Government Overreach

History is replete with examples of governments misusing financial systems to control populations.

- **Post-9/11 Financial Surveillance:** The U.S. government expanded its financial surveillance capabilities under the Patriot Act, using anti-terrorism as a pretext. Critics argue that these powers have been abused to monitor law-abiding citizens.
- **Canada's Freedom Convoy Protests (2022):** The Canadian government froze the bank accounts of protestors and donors, showcasing how financial systems can be weaponized against dissent.

A CBDC would amplify such powers exponentially, providing governments with real-time control over citizens' finances.

Arguments for Digital Currency (and Counterarguments)

Argument 1: Efficiency and Speed

Proponents argue that digital currencies enable faster and cheaper transactions. For example, international remittances can be processed in seconds, bypassing intermediaries.

Counterargument:

Cryptocurrencies and private payment systems already address this issue. Adopting a CBDC introduces risks without offering significant advantages over existing technologies like blockchain-based stablecoins or platforms like PayPal and Venmo.

Argument 2: Financial Inclusion
Supporters claim that CBDCs can provide unbanked populations with access to financial systems.

Counterargument:
Digital currencies require internet access and digital devices, which are unavailable to many unbanked individuals. Traditional solutions, such as mobile banking and microfinance, are more practical and proven alternatives.

Argument 3: Transparency and Fraud Prevention
CBDCs can reduce tax evasion and illicit activities by ensuring all transactions are traceable.

Counterargument:
While reducing fraud is important, the trade-off in privacy and freedom is unacceptable. Moreover, existing tools like blockchain analytics can address fraud without centralizing control.

The Path Forward: Safeguarding Financial Freedom
Instead of adopting a CBDC, the U.S. should focus on strengthening its existing financial systems and exploring private-sector innovations. Policymakers should prioritize:

- **Protecting Cash:** Ensuring that cash remains a viable option for all transactions.
- **Regulating Cryptocurrencies:** Creating a balanced regulatory framework that mitigates risks while fostering innovation.

⊚ **Enhancing Financial Education:** Empowering citizens to make informed choices about digital and traditional financial tools.

Conclusion

Digital currencies, particularly CBDCs, represent a double-edged sword. While they promise efficiency and inclusivity, the risks to privacy, financial autonomy, and societal stability outweigh the potential benefits. By resisting the push for a government-controlled digital currency, the U.S. can safeguard its foundational values of freedom and individual rights. In other words, it's the only way to keep the government out of your pocketbook and meddling in your business.

11

ELIMINATE THE DEPARTMENT OF EDUCATION

THE **U.S. DEPARTMENT OF EDUCATION (ED)** was established as a Cabinet-level agency on May 4, 1980, following the signing of the Department of Education Organization Act by President Jimmy Carter on October 17, 1979.

Its primary mission is to promote student achievement and preparation for global competitiveness by fostering educational excellence and ensuring equal access.

Budget and Funding

In **Fiscal Year (FY) 2024**, the Department of Education had a budget of approximately **$241.66 billion**, distributed among its various subcomponents.

This funding supports a wide range of programs, including grants to states and local educational agencies, student financial assistance, and educational research initiatives.

Employee Workforce

As of the latest available data, the Department employs around **4,400 individuals**. These employees are responsible for administering federal education programs, conducting research, and ensuring compliance with federal education laws.

Allocation of Funds

The Department's budget is allocated across several key areas:

- ⊚ **Elementary and Secondary Education:** Funds are provided to support K-12 education, particularly in high-poverty schools, to ensure all students have access to quality education.
- ⊚ **Higher Education:** Allocations support student financial aid programs, including Pell Grants and federal student loans, to make postsecondary education more accessible.
- ⊚ **Special Education:** Funding is directed toward programs that assist students with disabilities, ensuring they receive appropriate educational services.
- ⊚ **Educational Research and Improvement:** Investments are made in research initiatives aimed at improving educational practices and outcomes nationwide.

These allocations reflect the Department's commitment to enhancing educational opportunities and outcomes for all students across the United States.

The U.S. Department of Education (ED) has long been a controversial institution, seen by critics as a bloated federal bureaucracy with limited effectiveness in improving educational outcomes. Established in 1980, the ED was designed to centralize education policy, ensure equal access, and promote educational excellence. However, four decades of experience demonstrate that the department has fallen short of its goals, often overstepping its constitutional boundaries and entangling local schools in a web of regulations. Eliminating the Department of Education is not only a matter of efficiency but a step toward restoring local control, empowering parents, and ensuring that education serves the needs of students, not bureaucrats.

The Case Against the Department of Education

1. Federal Overreach

The U.S. Constitution does not grant the federal government authority over education; this responsibility historically rested with states and local communities. The establishment of the ED marked a significant expansion of federal control, infringing on the 10th Amendment. By dictating policies through conditional funding, the federal government has centralized decision-making, often ignoring regional and cultural differences in educational needs.

2. Declining Educational Outcomes

Despite trillions of dollars spent since the ED's inception, U.S. education outcomes have stagnated or declined compared to international standards. According to the National Assessment of Educational Progress (NAEP), proficiency levels in math and reading have seen minimal improvement over decades. Federal mandates such as No Child Left Behind (NCLB) and Common Core have created a compliance-driven system, prioritizing standardized testing over genuine learning and innovation.

3. Inefficiency and Bureaucracy

The ED employs over 4,000 people and administers an annual budget exceeding $240 billion. Yet, a significant portion of this budget is consumed by administrative costs and duplicative programs. Instead of directly supporting teachers and students, funds are often redirected toward fulfilling regulatory requirements and supporting redundant oversight mechanisms.

4. Stifling Parental Choice and Local Autonomy

Federal control over education has marginalized the role of parents and local communities. Initiatives like Common Core were implemented with minimal input from parents, educators, or local officials, leading to widespread dissatisfaction. This top-down approach has stifled school choice, innovation, and the ability of communities to tailor education to their unique needs.

The Benefits of Eliminating the Department of Education

1. Restoring Local Control

Education policy should reflect the values and needs of local communities. Eliminating the ED would return decision-making power to states, school districts, and parents, allowing them to design curricula, set standards, and allocate resources without federal interference.

2. Empowering Parents Through Choice

Without federal mandates dictating school policy, parents would have greater opportunities to choose schools that align with their values and priorities. School choice programs, including charter schools, vouchers, and homeschooling, would thrive in a decentralized education system.

3. Redirecting Funds to Classrooms

Eliminating the ED would free up billions of dollars currently spent on federal bureaucracy. These funds could be redirected to classrooms, where they would have a direct impact on teacher salaries, student resources, and infrastructure improvements.

4. Encouraging Innovation

States and localities are laboratories of democracy. By decentralizing education, states can experiment with innovative approaches to teaching, technology integration, and vocational training, creating models that other states can emulate.

Proposed Transition Plan

Eliminating the ED must be done thoughtfully to minimize disruption. The following steps outline a practical transition plan:

1. **Phase Out Federal Funding:** Transition federal education programs to state control over a five-year period. Federal grants can be converted into block grants, allowing states to allocate funds as they see fit.
2. **Repeal Federal Mandates:** Repeal laws like NCLB and Common Core, giving states the freedom to set their own standards and assessment methods.
3. **Strengthen Parental Rights:** Pass legislation to empower parents in making educational choices for their children, including expanding school choice programs and protecting homeschooling rights.
4. **Reduce Bureaucracy:** Gradually transfer oversight responsibilities to state education departments, ensuring a seamless handover of essential functions.
5. **Invest in Local Solutions:** Encourage states to use their newfound autonomy to invest in teacher training, technology, and community-driven initiatives.

Addressing Concerns

1. Equity

Critics argue that eliminating the ED could widen disparities in education quality between states. This concern can be addressed by establishing state-led partnerships and encouraging philanthropic investment in underserved areas.

2. Accountability

Decentralization does not mean abandoning accountability. States would remain accountable to their residents, who can demand transparency and results from local officials more effectively than from distant federal agencies.

3. Federal Oversight of Civil Rights

The ED's Office for Civil Rights enforces anti-discrimination laws in schools. These responsibilities could be transferred to the Department of Justice, ensuring civil rights protections without maintaining a separate education bureaucracy.

Conclusion

The U.S. Department of Education represents a failed experiment in federal control of education. Its elimination would not only save taxpayers billions but also restore the constitutional principle of local governance. By empowering states, parents, and teachers, we can create a more responsive, innovative, and effective education system that meets the diverse needs of American students. Education is too important to be left to Washington bureaucrats—it belongs in the hands of families and communities.

12

UNION INFLUENCE

THE HISTORY OF WORKERS' UNIONS IN the United States is deeply rooted in the industrial transformation of the 19th century, where laborers sought collective power to address the challenges of low wages, long hours, and unsafe working conditions. Early efforts to organize emerged in the 1830s with craft unions, which represented skilled workers like printers and shoemakers. These unions primarily focused on protecting their trades against the influx of unskilled laborers and the changing dynamics of industrialization. However, their influence was limited, as the U.S. economy relied heavily on a laissez-faire philosophy, and workers' rights were not yet recognized under the law.

The late 19th century saw the rise of influential labor organizations like the Knights of Labor, founded in 1869. Unlike earlier craft unions, the Knights of Labor sought to unite workers across trades, advocating for an eight-hour workday, equal pay for women, and the abolition of child labor. Their inclusive approach, however, faced significant resistance from industrialists and was often undermined by violent confrontations, such as the Haymarket Affair of 1886. This event, a peaceful rally turned violent due to a bomb explosion, marked a turning point for labor activism, associating unions with radicalism in the public mind.

The early 20th century brought about significant changes with the formation of the American Federation of Labor (AFL), founded by Samuel Gompers. Unlike the broad aims of the Knights of Labor, the AFL focused on "bread-and-butter" issues—wages, hours, and working conditions—and represented skilled laborers. The AFL's pragmatic approach made it one of the most enduring labor organizations in American history. In 1935, the Congress of Industrial Organizations (CIO) emerged, breaking away from the AFL to represent industrial workers in mass production industries like steel and auto manufacturing. This period was marked by successful strikes and union gains, bolstered by New Deal policies like the Wagner Act of 1935, which guaranteed workers the right to unionize and bargain collectively.

The question of whether the need for unions has outgrown itself is complex and context-dependent. While unions played a crucial role in establishing worker protections and improving labor conditions during the industrial era, many of the rights they once fought for are now enshrined in law. These include minimum wage laws, anti-discrimination statutes, workplace safety regulations, and protections against wrongful termination. Given this legal framework, some argue that unions have become less essential in their original role of safeguarding basic worker rights. However, the answer varies depending on the industry, region, and specific workplace dynamics.

Arguments That the Need for Unions Has Outgrown Itself

1. **Comprehensive Legal Protections**
   Modern labor laws, such as the Fair Labor Standards Act (FLSA), Occupational Safety and Health Act (OSHA), and Title VII of the Civil Rights Act, provide

robust protections for workers. These laws address many of the core issues unions historically fought for, including safe working conditions, wage equity, and protection from discrimination and harassment. With these safeguards in place, some argue that unions are no longer as critical for protecting workers' basic rights.

2. **Economic Burden on Employers and Consumers**
Unions can impose significant financial and operational burdens on businesses, including high wages, generous benefits, and restrictive work rules. These costs can reduce competitiveness, particularly in industries facing global competition, and can result in higher prices for consumers. Critics argue that unions sometimes prioritize their own interests over the sustainability of the businesses they represent.

3. **Focus on Outdated Practices**
Critics claim that unions often resist innovation and necessary reforms. For instance, union opposition to automation, flexible work arrangements, or merit-based pay can hinder progress and efficiency. This is particularly problematic in fast-evolving industries where adaptability is crucial.

4. **Public-Sector Union Challenges**
In the public sector, unions have been criticized for prioritizing employee benefits over the effective delivery of public services. For example, pensions and other long-term liabilities negotiated by public-sector unions have placed significant strain on government budgets, often at the expense of taxpayers.

Arguments for the Continued Relevance of Unions

1. **Wage Inequality and Job Security**
   Despite legal protections, wage inequality persists, and many workers still face job insecurity. Unions can play a vital role in advocating for fair wages, improved benefits, and protections against arbitrary layoffs, particularly in industries with low unionization and limited bargaining power.

2. **Advocating for Vulnerable Workers**
   In sectors like gig work or fast food, many workers are not covered by traditional labor protections or collective bargaining agreements. Unions can provide a voice for these employees, addressing issues such as wage theft, lack of benefits, and unsafe working conditions.

3. **Maintaining Worker Influence**
   Even with legal protections, workers often lack a voice in decisions that affect their daily lives, such as scheduling, workplace policies, and job restructuring. Unions provide a mechanism for workers to collectively advocate for their interests.

4. **Globalization and Outsourcing**
   In an increasingly globalized economy, jobs are often outsourced to countries with lower labor standards. Unions can help mitigate the impact on domestic workers by advocating for policies that protect local jobs and ensure fair treatment in international supply chains.

While many of the original functions of unions have been
absorbed by legal frameworks, there are still areas where
unions can provide value, particularly for vulnerable workers
and in industries without strong regulatory oversight. However,
unions must adapt to modern economic realities and focus on
collaboration, innovation, and accountability to remain relevant.
If they cling to outdated practices or pursue narrow self-inter-
ests, they risk becoming an obstacle to progress rather than
a force for positive change.

Unions reached their zenith in the mid-20th century, with
nearly one-third of American workers belonging to unions by
the 1950s. They played a critical role in shaping labor laws,
securing pensions, health benefits, and safer workplaces for
millions of workers. However, the latter half of the century saw
a decline in union membership, driven by globalization, the rise
of the service economy, and aggressive anti-union tactics by
employers. The 1980s marked a pivotal moment with President
Ronald Reagan's handling of the PATCO strike, signaling a shift
in federal attitudes toward unions.

Today, unions continue to advocate for workers, though
their membership and influence have diminished significantly.
Recent years have seen a resurgence of interest in unionization
in sectors like technology and retail, suggesting that the legacy
of collective labor power remains an essential aspect of the
American labor movement.

Workers' unions have historically played a significant role
in driving up the price of goods and services by influencing
wages, benefits, and workplace standards. While unions advocate for fair compensation and improved working conditions,
these gains often lead to increased labor costs for employers,
which are typically passed on to consumers. Below are several
key ways unions contribute to higher prices:

1. Increased Wages and Benefits

Unions negotiate higher wages and comprehensive benefits for their members, including healthcare, pensions, and paid leave. While these improvements enhance the quality of life for workers, they raise the overall cost of production. For industries with a strong union presence, such as manufacturing and construction, these additional costs are often reflected in the prices of goods and services.

2. Reduced Workplace Flexibility

Union contracts can impose rigid rules on how labor is managed, including limits on overtime, staffing requirements, and job classifications. This can lead to inefficiencies in operations, particularly in industries like transportation, education, and public utilities. For example, unionized workplaces might require higher staffing levels or prohibit certain cost-saving measures, increasing operational expenses and, ultimately, the prices consumers pay.

3. Costs of Strikes and Work Stoppages

Strikes or work stoppages, while a powerful tool for unions, can disrupt production and lead to significant financial losses for companies. To recover these costs, businesses often increase prices. For example, prolonged strikes in industries such as shipping or automotive manufacturing can cause supply chain delays, leading to higher prices for consumers due to limited supply.

4. Union Influence on Public Services

In sectors like education, healthcare, and public transportation, unionized labor often results in higher costs for taxpayers.

Public-sector unions negotiate for increased pay and benefits, which can strain municipal or state budgets. These higher costs are frequently passed on to citizens through increased taxes or higher fees for services like public transit or utilities.

5. Impacts on Competitiveness and Productivity

Union-driven wage increases can sometimes outpace productivity gains, making unionized businesses less competitive. For example, if union contracts require pay raises that are not matched by improvements in efficiency or output, businesses may face higher per-unit costs. In global markets, this can lead to higher prices as domestic businesses struggle to compete with lower-cost international producers.

Examples in Practice:

- ◉ **Automotive Industry:** In the mid-20th century, unions like the United Automobile Workers (UAW) secured high wages and extensive benefits for autoworkers. While these contracts provided financial security for millions, they also made American cars more expensive compared to foreign-made vehicles, contributing to the decline of U.S. automakers' global market share.
- ◉ **Public Utilities:** Utility companies often pass union-negotiated wage and pension costs onto consumers through higher rates, as seen in regulated energy and water markets.

While unions have undoubtedly improved working conditions and wages for many, the associated increases in labor costs highlight the delicate balance between supporting workers and managing the affordability of goods and services.

Teachers' unions, while originally established to protect the rights and working conditions of educators, have increasingly been criticized for prioritizing their own agendas over the well-being of students and the interests of taxpayers. Their influence on education policy, school funding, and labor negotiations has often come at the expense of academic outcomes, financial efficiency, and the needs of children and their families.

Hijacking Education

Teachers' unions have amassed significant political power, enabling them to shape education policies that often align with their interests rather than those of students. For example, unions frequently resist reforms such as school choice, merit-based pay for teachers, and standardized testing accountability measures, arguing that these initiatives undermine public education or teachers' job security. While these arguments may have some validity, they often ignore the broader need to improve student outcomes, leaving underperforming schools and teachers shielded from accountability. In some cases, union-backed policies have perpetuated a status quo where innovation and educational competition are stifled, trapping students in failing schools.

Burdening the Taxpayer

The financial demands of teachers' unions also place a heavy burden on taxpayers. Union negotiations often result in generous pension plans, healthcare benefits, and salary increases that far exceed those in the private sector. These agreements, while beneficial to educators, are funded by taxpayers, many of whom face their own financial challenges. In states with strong union influence, underfunded teacher pension systems have become a fiscal crisis, consuming resources that could otherwise be invested in classrooms or other public needs. Moreover, union-led strikes or threats of strikes frequently pressure local governments to acquiesce to demands, further escalating costs.

Neglecting Children's Needs

Perhaps most concerning is the degree to which unions have focused on protecting their members rather than advocating for policies that directly benefit students. For instance, unions often oppose policies that would make it easier to dismiss underperforming teachers, citing job security concerns. As a result, students are sometimes left with educators who fail to meet professional standards, disproportionately affecting children in underprivileged areas.

Additionally, during the COVID-19 pandemic, many teachers' unions resisted the reopening of schools, citing safety concerns, even when evidence suggested that in-person learning could resume safely. The prolonged closures had devastating consequences for students' mental health, social development, and academic progress, particularly for those from low-income families.

Conclusion

While teachers' unions have a legitimate role in advocating for educators, their actions often appear to prioritize their own interests over the broader mission of education: to prepare students for the future. Their resistance to reform, focus on financial gains, and neglect of student-centered policies highlight the need for a recalibration of priorities in American education. To truly serve children and communities, unions must embrace accountability, support innovation, and work collaboratively to ensure that every student has access to a high-quality education. Without these changes, the education system risks further decline, burdening taxpayers and failing the very individuals it was designed to serve.

13

IT'S ALL ABOUT THE ENERGY

**But Mostly Money and Power...
and not Climate Change**

I N AN ERA MARKED BY RAPIDLY shifting energy landscapes and growing environmental concerns, understanding the extent of a nation's energy reserves—and how long those reserves might sustain its consumption patterns—is paramount. The United States, long recognized as a global energy powerhouse, possesses a diverse mix of fossil fuel resources that have driven its economic growth and technological innovation for decades. Yet when we examine the scale and sustainability of these reserves in a comparative global framework, a complex picture emerges.

I believe it's important to highlight this, especially since whenever someone asks the president about lowering costs, President Trump consistently points to energy as the starting point. And for good reason—it's all about energy, plain and simple. The United States has abundant energy resources, and utilizing them has a far smaller impact on climate change compared to countries like China and India. Even if we devoted our entire tax base to eliminating and reversing climate change, we would end up bankrupt, while nations that made no such financial sacrifice would gain a strategic advantage over us. Donald J. Trump understands this entirely, while other leaders position themselves to pander to a narrative and not economic realities.

The U.S. Energy Landscape in Numbers

The United States stands as a formidable player in the global energy arena, underpinned by a diverse mix of fossil fuel reserves. To understand the country's long-term energy security, we begin by examining the key figures:

- **Oil Reserves:**
  The U.S. has proven oil reserves in the vicinity of **40–45 billion barrels**. Although this figure is robust, it represents only a modest share of global oil reserves. For context, major oil-producing nations such as Saudi Arabia and Venezuela hold around **260 billion** and **300 billion barrels**, respectively. This disparity highlights that while the U.S. is a significant producer, its oil reserves are relatively limited when compared globally.

- **Natural Gas Reserves:**
  With proven natural gas reserves estimated at **450–500 trillion cubic feet (TCF)**, the U.S. maintains a strong position in the natural gas market. However, it still trails behind countries like Russia, which boasts reserves exceeding **1,600 TCF**. The U.S. figures demonstrate a competitive but not dominant share of the world's natural gas resources.

- **Coal Reserves:**
  Coal is an area where the United States truly excels. Possessing approximately **250–300 billion short tons** of coal, the U.S. holds roughly **25–30%** of the world's recoverable coal reserves. This abundance of coal not only diversifies the nation's energy portfolio but also

provides a solid buffer in terms of long-term energy supply.

Energy Longevity: How Long Can Our Reserves Last?

Assessing how long these reserves could last requires comparing current consumption rates with the available resources. While consumption figures vary by fuel type and over time, a few key points can be drawn:

- ⊚ **Oil and Natural Gas:**
  Despite high levels of production, the relatively smaller proportion of proven oil and natural gas reserves means that, under current consumption trends, these fuels could face supply constraints sooner than coal. The U.S. has optimized its extraction technologies, notably with advancements like hydraulic fracturing, also known as fracking, to extend the life of these reserves. Nevertheless, the finite nature of these resources continues to pose long-term challenges.

- ⊚ **Coal:**
  Given the sheer volume of coal reserves, coal remains a substantial energy buffer. If current usage patterns persist, the U.S. could theoretically rely on its coal reserves for many decades. However, environmental concerns and the global push toward decarbonization have accelerated discussions about reducing coal dependency.

Alternative Energy Sources: A Comparison

Despite significant progress in renewable energy technologies—such as solar, wind, and hydroelectric power—their current contributions do not yet match the scale and reliability of fossil fuels. Renewable energy sources, while promising for the future, face several limitations:

- **Intermittency and Storage:**
  Unlike fossil fuels, which offer a steady and storable energy supply, renewables are often intermittent, relying on weather conditions and time of day. Although battery storage and grid management technologies are evolving, they have not yet reached a point where renewables can fully substitute for the consistent energy output provided by oil, natural gas, and coal.

- **Infrastructure and Investment:**
  Transitioning from an energy system built around fossil fuels to one dominated by renewables involves massive infrastructural overhauls. Despite aggressive investments, the scale of the current fossil fuel reserves—backed by decades of development and optimization—remains unmatched by alternative energy capacities.

So why does the progressive left like to demonize fossil fuels and their fellow citizens who continue to consume them? Narrative?

Political Narratives and the Energy Debate

In the contemporary discourse on energy policy, the narrative surrounding fossil fuels and renewables is highly polarized. A recurring theme in political debates is the portrayal of fossil fuels as inherently detrimental, with a focus on their environmental impact and finite nature. Some commentators, particularly on the political left, argue that continued reliance on fossil fuels perpetuates environmental degradation and undermines the urgent need to transition to greener alternatives.

However, such narratives often understate the quantitative reality of the U.S. energy portfolio. The figures—**40-45 billion barrels of oil, 450-500 TCF of natural gas, and 250-300 billion short tons of coal**—demonstrate that the United States has a significant and diverse energy reserve that currently fuels its economic and industrial strength. While it is imperative to address environmental concerns and invest in renewable technologies, dismissing the robustness of our fossil fuel reserves ignores the pragmatic realities of today's energy consumption and production.

I contend that while renewable energy is crucial for the long-term sustainability of our energy systems, it is premature to suggest that alternative energy sources can immediately replace the depth and reliability of the United States' fossil fuel reserves. A balanced view that recognizes both the potential of renewables and the current indispensability of fossil fuels is essential. Only by integrating this balanced perspective can policymakers chart a course that ensures energy security, economic stability, and environmental responsibility. The United States must fully leverage its vast energy resources to maintain its competitive edge on the global stage and prevent economic decline caused by an overreliance on costly alternative energy sources.

Progressives push for limitless taxpayer spending in a futile attempt to outpace the world, all based on a climate narrative that is neither accurate nor sustainable. The left wing of the Democratic Party fails to see the bigger picture. As I've pointed out before, these are the same people who would have burned you at the stake for saying the world is round—only to laugh about it a century later. Their short-sightedness is dangerous. They manipulate public fear to control the narrative and fiscal policy, and if left unchecked, they will drive the nation into bankruptcy.

Tapping into our energy reserves is the only way to stabilize prices and prevent inflation from spiraling out of control. It's also baffling that every time a storm hits, left-wing politicians rush to the cameras, blaming it on climate change without presenting any real scientific evidence. These shortsighted, narrow-minded claims are not only reckless but also reveal a willingness to pander to an audience that may not question their narrative. Credibility has taken a back seat to fearmongering and tactics reminiscent of a snake oil salesman. They create urgency and fear to drive a consensus and then throw dollars at a problem... Ironically, it was a problem they created and now seem to have the magic elixir to fix it.

President Trump recognizes this issue and the simplicity of the left-wing argument. In fact, he's the only president in my lifetime who seems unconcerned with how any particular group perceives him. Ironically, Donald J. Trump has governed as a populist, and I believe his stance on climate change aligns with the views of the majority of voters. The problem, however, is that the media has never accurately reflected the sentiments of the silent majority. As I pointed out earlier, the media is overwhelmingly biased in its political leanings. If one relied solely on the mainstream media, they might believe the entire world opposes logic and common sense.

This ideology has permeated every aspect of our lives. Children are indoctrinated with these falsehoods by their teachers, while Hollywood reinforces them endlessly in its productions. Everywhere you turn, flawed life lessons are being pushed. It seems as though the narrative holds more power than actual science, and when anyone dares to challenge it, they are met with hostility, labeled, and effectively silenced by those who are beholden to it.

Many politicians understand this tactic—they create a sense of urgency, much like a skilled salesperson, but they stop short of asking for the sale. Instead, they prefer to manipulate through guilt, and their supporters eagerly follow along, feeling compelled to do so to justify their cause, reinforce their narrative, and abandon logic when necessary.

It's fascinating to live in an era where social media makes everything public, allowing past statements to be scrutinized as a measure of one's character and judgment. Yet, I watch as these individuals reflexively oppose anything related to Trump, regardless of merit. Their willingness to discard reason just to take an opposing stance is both transparent and unbecoming, causing them to lose credibility—at least in my eyes—daily.

I've observed how leftist policies consistently lead to higher costs for goods and services. Their energy policies contradict fundamental principles of both micro and macroeconomics, yet they divert attention elsewhere to avoid accountability. The left follows a strict playbook, relying on a segment of the population that prefers to follow rather than think critically. They continue to exploit uninformed voters because, at the core, their agenda is driven by money and power—not by genuinely serving the people.

14

DÉJÀ VU

THERE ARE COUNTLESS CHALLENGES FACING OUR country today, and I could write endlessly about them. Many of these issues have been debated for decades, while newer, socially driven topics—largely distractions, in my view—have taken center stage in recent years. While social issues dominate polling among the progressive left, the reality is that the country doesn't function based on them. The media has conditioned many to echo the narrative, diverting attention from what truly matters: enacting real, fundamental change that benefits every citizen within our borders. Look at what the conservatives were trying to fix just a little over 30 years ago in what was called, The Contract with America!

The **Contract with America**, introduced by Republicans in the U.S. House of Representatives during the 1994 midterm elections, was a legislative agenda aimed at promoting conservative values and policy changes. Spearheaded by **Newt Gingrich** and other GOP leaders, it outlined 10 key proposals that Republicans promised to bring to a vote within the first 100 days of taking control of the House.

Main Items in the Contract with America

1. **The Fiscal Responsibility Act**
   - Proposed a balanced budget amendment to the Constitution.

- Called for a line-item veto to give the President power to remove specific spending items.
- Advocated for limitations on tax increases.

2. **The Taking Back Our Streets Act**
   - Focused on crime reduction.
   - Included provisions for more prisons, stricter penalties, and support for local law enforcement.
   - Advocated for the "truth in sentencing" to ensure criminals served their full terms.

3. **The Personal Responsibility Act**
   - Sought to reform welfare programs.
   - Proposed stricter eligibility requirements for government assistance.
   - Aimed to reduce dependency on welfare and promote work requirements.

4. **The Family Reinforcement Act**
   - Advocated for family-friendly policies, such as child support enforcement.
   - Proposed tax incentives for adoption.
   - Encouraged reforms to strengthen traditional family structures.

5. **The American Dream Restoration Act**
   - Proposed a $500 per child tax credit for families.
   - Sought to reduce the marriage penalty in the tax code.
   - Advocated for greater family financial stability.

6. **The National Security Restoration Act**
   - Emphasized stronger defense spending and policies.
   - Called for reducing U.S. dependence on the United Nations for foreign policy decisions.
   - Promoted military readiness and sovereignty.

7. **The Senior Citizens' Fairness Act**
   - Proposed changes to Social Security to increase earnings limits for retirees.
   - Advocated for repealing tax increases on Social Security benefits implemented earlier.
   - Strengthened retirement security.

8. **The Job Creation and Wage Enhancement Act**
   - Focused on economic growth and deregulation.
   - Included tax cuts for capital gains.
   - Reduced regulatory burdens to encourage entrepreneurship and investment.

9. **The Common Sense Legal Reform Act**
   - Sought to address perceived abuses in the legal system.
   - Proposed limits on punitive damages in lawsuits.
   - Advocated for reforms to reduce frivolous litigation.

10. **The Citizen Legislature Act**
   - Aimed to establish term limits for members of Congress.
   - Promoted the idea of a citizen-led government to prevent career politicians from dominating Congress.

Impact of the Contract with America

◉ In the **1994 elections**, the Republican Party gained control of the House for the first time in 40 years.
◉ Several items from the Contract were introduced, debated, and passed in the House, though not all became law.
◉ The Contract's focus on clear policy goals and accountability is credited with reshaping American politics and increasing public engagement.

I bring this up because many of the ideas presented in this book are not new—they've been discussed for decades. While the *Contract with America* introduced some reforms, many were merely temporary fixes, such as tax credits and raising earning limits for seniors. The more impactful proposals, like term limits and other long-term structural changes, were never enacted. A true solution, such as abolishing the tax code and transitioning to a tariff-based system or a combination of tariffs and a VAT system, would address the core issues that led to the need for the contract in the first place. Though the *Contract with America* sounded promising at the time, it lacked the boldness necessary to enact lasting change. The reality is, we've been grappling with these challenges for decades.

As of early 2025, various polls have identified the following top political issues among Americans:

1. **The Economy:** Consistently a primary concern, with 81% of registered voters in 2024 stating it was very important to their presidential vote.

2. **Inflation and Prices:** A survey from October 2024 found that 24% of Americans considered inflation and prices as the most important issue.

3. **Immigration:** Approximately half of U.S. adults in December 2024 identified immigration and border issues as key concerns for 2025, up from one-third the previous year.

4. **Health Care:** A significant issue for many voters, with 76% of Harris supporters in 2024 citing it as very important to their vote.

5. **Supreme Court Appointments:** In 2024, 73% of Harris supporters considered the types of Supreme Court justices the candidates would pick as very important.

6. **Abortion:** The importance of abortion as a voting issue increased notably after the Supreme Court's decision to overturn Roe v. Wade, with 67% of Harris supporters in 2024 stating it was very important to their vote.

7. **Crime and Criminal Justice Reform:** A key concern for many voters, with 76% of Trump supporters in 2024 citing violent crime as very important to their vote.

8. **Climate Change and the Environment:** An important issue for many voters, with 50% of voters in 2024 considering climate change as extremely or very important to their presidential vote choice.

9. **Education:** A significant concern for voters, with 68% of Harris supporters in 2024 stating it was very important to their vote.

10. **Taxes and Government Spending:** A notable issue for many voters, with 61% of Trump supporters in 2024 considering taxes as very important to their vote.

These priorities can vary based on political affiliation, with Republicans often emphasizing the economy, immigration, and crime, while Democrats may focus more on health care, Supreme Court appointments, and abortion.

The stark contrast between political parties and the issues they prioritize reveals much about how leaders are chosen. I once heard Governor Chris Christie describe the cyclical shifts in New Jersey's leadership, where voters typically elect a Republican governor for two terms, followed by a Democrat. He explained it this way: *"Voters grow weary of the chaos and games, so they elect the adults to restore order and prosperity. After a period of stability, they tire of being told what to do and opt for a more liberal approach. When chaos inevitably follows, they put the adults back in charge."*

While I wasn't the biggest fan of the Governor because I didn't believe he was a true conservative, he did make some great points with his statement. He was referencing the pendulum which makes wild swings with middle-of-the-road voters. The middle is what decides elections, and when policies start to affect those middle-of-the-road voters, they will start to look for an alternative to whoever is in power.

This pattern perfectly reflects what happened during the Biden administration. Left unchecked, Biden's policies led to record-breaking border crossings, the worst inflation in over 40 years, and an economy in a constant state of uncertainty. Frustrated by the disorder, the American people elected a leader who follows through on his promises and communicates his plans transparently.

The real issue, once again, is the media. Rather than holding the administration accountable, they focus on "gotcha" moments and distort policy initiatives. Donald J. Trump is delivering exactly what he campaigned on, yet the media and progressive left act as if his policies are unexpected or radical. They would gain more credibility by acknowledging that the majority of voters chose this path. Americans are tired of being put last and deceived—now, they are demanding real leadership.

The real challenge is that the political pendulum will inevitably swing back. No matter how successful the administration is or how much prosperity the country experiences, we have only one opportunity to restore America and secure its future. If the Democratic Party doesn't undergo a radical shift, another progressive leader will eventually emerge. It's only a matter of time before a new administration seeks to undo the progress we achieve.

Those who have lived through multiple presidencies understand that the window for enacting lasting, fundamental change is small. Temporary fixes, like executive orders, won't suffice. We must pass new laws and potentially even constitutional amendments to ensure these reforms are permanent and not easily reversed by future Congresses or administrations.

You might be wondering why I haven't dedicated a section of this book to discussing border security. But for those who think logically, this should be a no-brainer. A country cannot exist without borders. While some argue that borders are racist or try to attach every other "-ist" label to them, the reality is that we have allowed unchecked entry—including criminals—into our country throughout the entirety of the Biden administration. Frankly, it's incomprehensible.

This situation reminds me of the "broken windows" theory, which suggests that when a community is visibly neglected—riddled with broken windows and signs of decay—residents lose their sense of pride, and that mentality spreads, leading to further decline. The border crisis reflects the same phenomenon.

When we stop enforcing immigration laws, disregard national security, and allow crime to spiral out of control, the rest of the country follows suit.

I fully support legal immigration—after all, we are a nation built by immigrants. My great-grandparents came to America from Italy and Hungary, embracing the dream of freedom and opportunity. The United States is a true melting pot, shaped by those seeking a better life. However, I believe that in our relatively short lifespans, many fail to recognize the gradual erosion of our fundamental freedoms. Since the country's founding, we have been surrendering them piece by piece. This includes excessive taxation, far beyond what the Founders intended, restrictions on free speech, and a reckless disregard for securing our borders.

When you step back and consider everything we've discussed, it becomes nearly impossible to argue against these proposals. Who would oppose lowering taxes, living within our means, spending only what we can afford, ensuring safe streets, or securing our elections to prevent fraud? Who would reject a merit-based system that upholds integrity over mediocrity? And who would willingly surrender their fundamental right to free speech? The truth is, no rational person wakes up and says, "I'd love to give more of my hard-earned money to the government."

Yet, the arguments coming from the left often defy logic. Many of their positions are not only absurd but also deliberately misleading. They've conditioned their supporters to follow along without question, repeating talking points rather than engaging in meaningful discussion. Of course, they'll claim the same about conservatives, but I've witnessed the difference firsthand as a consultant for many years.

Just recently, my stepson and I attended a political meeting with a group of young conservatives. I sat back and listened as they passionately debated real issues—bills, policies, and legislation from the national level down to local governance. These were thoughtful, informed discussions about the future of our country. Meanwhile, the radical left remains stuck on the same tired narrative: "Orange Man Bad." While conservatives are analyzing tax policies and their long-term impact, the left is fixated on distractions.

It's time to recognize the truth: they were never interested in working with us. They don't want compromise; they want control. Their arguments aren't grounded in logic but in emotional manipulation. We could waste endless energy refuting their baseless accusations—denying that we're racist, misogynist, or the second coming of a 1930s dictator—but that's exactly what they want. Their strategy is to deflect and distract, keeping us off message until election time so they can cling to power.

It's no coincidence that the progressive left refuses to address the issues outlined in this work. They avoid real solutions because their power depends on division and chaos. They don't want to fix these problems—they want to exploit them. It's time we stopped playing their game and started taking back control of the conversation.

I firmly believe we have only one chance to save America, and that time is now. For the first time in my life, I'm witnessing a movement that refuses to settle for temporary fixes that can be undone in the next political cycle. We finally have a president who not only brings a lifetime of business experience to the table, but who also gained invaluable insight during his first term in office. After stepping away, he had the opportunity to see firsthand the extent of lawfare and policies designed to harm, rather than help, the American people.

This is our moment to fundamentally restore and strengthen our nation—for ourselves, our children, and future generations. We must tune out the distractions and remain laser-focused on implementing policies that create a fair and prosperous America. These policies will benefit all Americans, even those who oppose them—they just don't realize it yet.

We must stand with President Trump, ignore the noise, and hold this administration accountable. And we cannot allow them to lose sight of why we elected them in the first place. The American people are fed up with the corruption and chaos, and we are ready to fight for our freedoms. If we don't act now, I fear we may never get another chance. We must do everything in our power to put these policies into action—because I truly believe this is the Only Way to Save America!

15

ONE CHANCE FOR THE REPUBLIC

EVERY WEEKDAY AT AROUND 7:30 AM Eastern, I begin prepping my morning show, **The Mike Schwartz Show**, and there's never a shortage of news to cover. Since Donald J. Trump won back the White House, waking up every day feels like Christmas morning. As I scan the headlines, there's always some breaking story about what this administration is accomplishing—almost as if a magic wand has been waved to bring common sense back to America. By the time I begin preparing my evening show, **2 Mikes Live** at 4:00 PM, the entire news cycle has turned over. It's as if the Trump administration is moving at lightning speed, keeping the left off balance, preventing them from formulating arguments, let alone a strategy. Before they can organize their next protest outside a government building, another bombshell announcement sends them into yet another meltdown.

This is a brilliant strategic move by the Trump administration—it leaves little time for Democrats to adjust. Without even knowing what the next four years will bring, I can already predict, with great accuracy, how the Democratic Party will react to Donald Trump. At this point, they're no different from the insurance industry, operating under a familiar motto: **delay, deny, and defend**. They will delay appointments, obstruct bills, and stall every possible effort this administration makes. They will deny reality, deny science, and reject logic—even when the truth is staring them in the face. And they will defend the indefensible, all in a desperate bid to stop any conservative progress. It doesn't matter if a policy benefits the entire country—if it's not their idea, they are against it. While a handful of moderates may waver after facing backlash from their districts, the majority of them are so deep in the swamp they rarely engage with their own constituents.

Politics today resembles a sci-fi horror movie, where we're all screaming at the clueless characters to avoid disaster, but they charge right into it anyway. You'll see media pundits, left-wing activists, and Democrat politicians railing against everything this administration does—often defying basic logic. They rely on the fact that most Americans are too busy to look past the headlines, and they know the retractions and corrections are buried where no one will see them. Their strategy is predictable: accuse their opponents of the very thing they are guilty of, then sit back as their opponents waste time defending themselves instead of staying on message. It's an old playbook, but it still works. The politically savvy see through it, but the rest of America—either too distracted or too naive—falls for it every time. It's a manipulative, calculated tactic designed to exploit the weak and uninformed. That may sound harsh, but the truth isn't always easy to hear.

Have you ever tried debating a progressive? It's pointless. Most don't even understand what the word *progressive* actually means in the political context. It doesn't mean "progress"—it means moving away from the Constitution. Conservatism, on the other hand, is about preserving the founding values of this country. While no document is perfect, the genius of the Constitution lies in its built-in mechanisms for change. Yet progressives—many of whom have never even read it—insist it must be rewritten. Arguing with them is like trying to reason with a child throwing a tantrum over a toy they don't even understand.

Their nonsense is amplified on social media, where they spew generalized talking points while ignoring facts, figures, and, most importantly, logic. Take their outrage over Elon Musk investigating government waste. They should be celebrating transparency, yet they're up in arms simply because someone outside their establishment is exposing corruption. But as I mentioned earlier, nearly 40% of Americans don't pay income taxes at all—so they have no personal stake in how taxpayer money is spent. Their go-to argument? *"Musk isn't an elected official."* Guess what? Neither are the bureaucrats running these agencies, nor was Jack Smith, nor Bill Gates, nor the countless other unelected figures who influence policy. Their arguments are paper-thin, yet they keep making them, wasting everyone's time in a never-ending cycle of obstruction. This is what I meant about delay, it's all they know how to do.

Eventually, things will work themselves out, but not before the progressive machine has done its best to grind everything to a halt. They don't argue because they believe in anything; they argue because they *must*, just to keep up appearances. Their entire political survival depends on manufacturing outrage. Without it, their power crumbles. God forbid they pick their battles instead of acting like a toddler who just had their candy taken away. For those of us who genuinely care about this country—who actually understand the issues and want to fix the mess—we are beyond frustrated listening to these fools. But we know exactly how they will react because human nature doesn't change, and neither has their tired, recycled playbook over the last 20 years.

The time Trump spent out of the White House between terms may have been the most valuable years of his political career. Many are calling this new administration "Trump 2.0," and it's clear that witnessing the lies, corruption, and incompetence firsthand has sharpened the movement for this new era. Imagine if Trump had won in 2020—yes, we were making progress, but nothing compared to the momentum we see now. The urgency and efficiency with which this administration is addressing issues is staggering. Trump listened to the American people, and like a great quarterback adjusting at halftime, he restructured his game plan, fired up his team, and returned to the field determined to win. The extreme leftward shift under Biden made Trump's return inevitable. I truly believe he has a long-term vision for America's future, and that's why I support him. The American people seem to agree—his policy approval ratings were through the roof just one month into office.

Yet, his critics remain fixated on the same divisive distractions. They obsess over transgender issues, claiming that the administration's policies somehow threaten LGBTQ rights or harm race relations—right out of their tired old playbook. The irony is that during Trump's first term, his team would sometimes respond to these attacks in an effort to appear understanding. In Trump 2.0, there's no more playing defense. These narratives are nothing more than political tactics, and the people pushing them were never going to support him anyway. Trump is leading for all Americans, but that means embracing meritocracy—not picking winners and losers. The left's entire ideology contradicts itself: they claim to fight discrimination while actively creating it. They label their opponents as racists, sexists, or whatever new term they invent, all while engaging in the very behavior they condemn. Their hypocrisy is crystal clear.

For too long, conservatives have avoided direct confrontations, assuming that the Constitution and rule of law would ultimately prevail. But we can no longer afford to sit back and hope for common sense to win the day. We must be vocal, we must fight, and we must defend our freedoms—because the other side is aggressively working to dismantle them. They sell false promises of utopia while peddling fear and division, preying on the naive just to maintain power. Let's not forget that these same people oppose term limits for a reason. They've built a system where they don't have to live under the same rules as the rest of us. They enjoy exclusive healthcare, special retirement benefits, and a luxurious standard of living—because they rigged the system for themselves. Congress, as a whole, is complicit, and some so-called conservatives will inevitably be swept away when the dust settles.

When Elon Musk announced that he would investigate how certain members of Congress amassed vast wealth while earning less than $200,000 a year, the silent majority finally said, "It's about time!" Suddenly, some of the loudest voices in Congress went silent, while others—who once praised Musk—turned against him. Why? Because Musk isn't a threat to the country; he's a threat to the establishment. He isn't concerned with your Social Security number or tax returns, like the 100,000 unelected IRS employees who have access to them without accountability. The real issue is that he's exposing a corrupt system that benefits the ruling class while the American people pay the price.

The hard truth is that most of the people who make up the bureaucracy don't care because it's not their money. It's like going to the casino and the house giving you a thousand dollars to play with. You will most likely gamble it all away because you have no skin in the game. There are also those who would immediately cash it in and go home, figuring they got one over on the casino, but my point here is about human nature. Human nature doesn't change, and human nature makes humans pre-dictable. The way Trump 2.0 could go is ultimately predictable based on what we've witnessed from our government through-out our lifetimes. Promises made, promises overlooked and much more of the same old same old... However, Trump is different. We witnessed that in his first term, but the "break" changed things for the better.

If you're a business owner, part of an organization, someone with multiple careers, or a person who has felt the weight of government bureaucracy, the ideas in this book will likely res-onate with you more than with those who are out of touch or lack real-world experience. At the same time, plenty of people in this country glance at their pay stubs every other week and think, "Wow, they really took a big chunk," or "Who the heck is FICA?" It's up to those of us with a bit more life experience to help them understand the complexities of policies and proce-dures. These individuals may sense their freedoms are slipping away but haven't yet grasped the full scope of what's hap-pening to our country. If we don't push back, the very system they resent will continue working against them, shaping future leaders through corruption and control.

My stepson is in college now, and every semester, without fail, he comes home with stories about a new professor. It doesn't matter which class—it's always the same. There's bound to be a mask-wearing, woke, tenured professor who has spent their entire life in academia. Degrees don't automatically make someone intelligent or well-rounded. I say that knowing I have several myself, but my exposure to common sense started long before college. I didn't begin my college journey until I was 26. By then, I had already spent nine years in business, graduated from flight school, and started working on political campaigns. That's when I got my first real taste of how the political machine operates. Before I knew it, I was running campaigns, drafting policy, and writing speeches for candidates—driven by optimism and a deep love for my country.

It didn't take long for me to realize that the real problem wasn't just the people in the system—it was the system itself. While individuals are naturally shaped by human nature, the structure they operate within has become inherently flawed. What began with noble and altruistic intentions has slowly crumbled under the crushing weight of excessive bureaucracy, piling up year after year. The system is teetering on the brink of collapse due to several key factors: a lack of transparency, expanding regulatory overreach, and a financial framework completely disconnected from the principles of responsible household management.

How could we, as Americans, expect our elected representatives to be responsible stewards of our hard-earned tax dollars when they are not bound by the same financial realities as the rest of us? They operate in a world vastly different from ours, yet we still expect them to understand our struggles. While this issue exists at state and local levels, it is nowhere near as severe as what we witness in the federal government. It's time to restore balance—to return to the principles the Founders originally envisioned. We must eliminate waste, fraud, and abuse while ensuring future administrations can't simply undo the progress by slipping back into the same dysfunctional patterns. Those who have been feasting off the system will do everything in their power to keep their gravy train running, dismissing any real reform with the usual "nothing to see here." But we can't afford to let them continue unchecked.

Trump 2.0 appears ready to implement lasting change—change that could steer the country back on track for the long haul. That is, unless we allow the noise to drown out basic logic and common sense. The left will relentlessly attempt to obstruct our agenda, even when our policies benefit the nation. The best strategy? Tune them out. If we stay focused, work tirelessly, and push forward, we can pull the country back from the brink of bankruptcy and collapse. We are in the midst of an almost 250-year experiment—young compared to civilizations with thousands of years of history. The United States once stood as the world's strongest nation, but reckless decisions have buried us in debt and brought us dangerously close to ruin. The COVID-19 pandemic put us to the test, and the left's response left us in an even more precarious position. We witnessed one of the greatest wealth transfers in history—one that bypassed the middle class entirely.

While small businesses were forced to shut down under government-imposed lockdowns, major corporations—especially Big Tech, Big Pharma, and e-commerce giants—thrived. Companies like Amazon, Apple, Microsoft, and Google saw record-breaking profits as consumers shifted to online shopping and remote work. Pharmaceutical giants such as Pfizer and Moderna raked in billions from government-funded vaccine contracts. Meanwhile, the Federal Reserve injected trillions into the economy through stimulus measures, inflating stock prices and disproportionately benefiting the wealthy, who own the majority of stock market assets. While Wall Street boomed, Main Street suffered, with many working and middle-class Americans losing jobs or experiencing stagnant wages.

Government stimulus checks offered temporary relief but fueled long-term inflation. Everyday Americans saw their purchasing power diminish as prices soared, while asset-holders—the wealthy—watched their real estate and investments skyrocket in value. The Paycheck Protection Program (PPP), meant to support small businesses, was heavily exploited by large corporations, celebrities, and fraudsters, while many genuine small business owners struggled to access funds. Lockdowns and restrictions forced hundreds of thousands of small businesses to shut down permanently, further con- solidating market share among corporate giants. As a result, wealth concentration surged as mom-and-pop shops couldn't compete with big-box retailers that were allowed to stay open.

Low interest rates and massive liquidity injections triggered a real estate surge, pricing out many first-time homebuy- ers, while institutional investors like BlackRock scooped up properties. The rental market became even more expensive, worsening the financial strain on lower-income Americans.

Government-enforced shutdowns left millions reliant on unemployment benefits, stimulus checks, and rent moratori- ums—while those in power used the crisis to justify expanding government control. The bottom line? COVID-19 exacerbated wealth inequality. Billionaires gained trillions, corporate behe- moths expanded their dominance, and the middle class was squeezed even further. The long-term consequences—espe- cially rising inflation and worsening housing affordability—are still being felt today.

Sounds good? Hardly. The takeaway here is clear: when the government gets involved, it rarely makes things better. As Ronald Reagan famously warned, the nine most terrifying words in the English language are: "I'm from the government, and I'm here to help." Advocates of big government ignore history and fail to learn from their mistakes. Many of us often refer to the definition of insanity—repeating the same actions while expecting different results. The left rarely deviates from its established approach, even when confronted with undeni- able evidence that their policies not only fail but actively harm the country.

It's time for a new direction, and anyone thinking rationally would agree. However, if I were to say that this new approach aligns with Donald J. Trump's vision, those afflicted with TDS on the left would instantly reject it, doing everything possible to obstruct progress. They just don't get it, and I fear they never will.

I have never seen anything like the MAGA movement in my lifetime. The enthusiasm, passion, and determination behind it are unparalleled. Never before have I witnessed such a powerful push to restore and improve our nation. We have one opportunity to get this right. The time is now. The leader is Donald J. Trump. And we must stand strong to secure the future of our great nation for generations to come.

This is *The Only Way to Save America*—let's not mess it up!

CLIFF NOTES

Chapter by Chapter

CHAPTER 1: A MANDATE STARTS THE CLOCK

Trump's Historic Victory

1. Donald J. Trump's 2024 victory was a **historic political moment**, making him only the second U.S. president to serve **non-consecutive terms**, following Grover Cleveland. This rare feat solidified his **resilient appeal** to the American electorate.
2. Trump won the **highest popular vote total** ever recorded for a Republican presidential candidate, **approximately 76 million votes**, signaling widespread support for his policies despite relentless media opposition.
3. The Republican Party gained **control of the White House, Senate, and House**, a rare political alignment that presented a significant opportunity to implement **sweeping legislative reforms** without immediate obstruction from Democratic leadership.
4. Trump's campaign made **unexpected gains** with **Middle Eastern and Muslim voters**, particularly in **Michigan**, marking a shift in political alignment due to growing concerns over progressive policies that many in these communities found socially and economically harmful.

Why Middle America Woke Up

1. Under the Biden-Harris administration, **economic conditions worsened significantly**, with inflation reaching historic highs, gas prices becoming unbearable for the working class, and supply chain disruptions creating unnecessary hardship for average Americans.
2. **Progressive distractions**, such as media-fueled hysteria over so-called "Project 2025," failed to sway voters, as everyday Americans prioritized **tangible economic issues** over speculative narratives and ideological fearmongering.
3. The **Democratic establishment ignored the concerns of working-class Americans**, focusing instead on policies that benefited corporate elites, special interest groups, and radical activists rather than addressing the needs of ordinary citizens.
4. Many voters began to realize that their **freedoms were being systematically eroded**, with government overreach extending into their personal lives, businesses, and constitutional rights, prompting a backlash at the ballot box.

Challenges Facing Trump 2.0

1. Trump faces a **limited window of time** to enact meaningful reforms, as history shows that **political momentum typically fades** within 18–24 months of a new administration. Without swift action, opposition forces will find ways to stall progress.
2. **Legal battles and assassination attempts** have demonstrated the extreme lengths to which Trump's adversaries are willing to go to prevent him from succeeding. This political warfare is unprecedented in modern American history.
3. The **mainstream media remains hostile**, fabricating misleading narratives and distorting policy successes to discredit Trump's administration and diminish public support.
4. **Congressional bureaucracy remains an obstacle**, as even with Republican control, **establishment politicians** may hesitate to support Trump's aggressive reform agenda, fearing backlash from special interest groups.

The Urgency of Reform

1. Trump's **second term represents the last viable opportunity** to make permanent structural changes to American governance, as a future administration may undo reforms if they are not deeply entrenched.
2. The **national debt has become a ticking time bomb**, with reckless spending putting America on the brink of fiscal disaster, requiring **bold and immediate action** to prevent economic collapse.
3. **Government overreach has reached critical levels**, impacting personal freedoms, business regulations, and state sovereignty—issues that must be addressed before they become irreversible.
4. **Temporary policy adjustments will not be enough**; instead, America needs deep, structural reform that prevents future administrations from reversing progress with the stroke of a pen.
5. If meaningful change is not implemented **within the first two years of Trump's second term**, political resistance will make it nearly impossible to accomplish the necessary legislative goals.

Chapter 2: A New Tax System

The Problem with the Federal Income Tax

1. The **federal income tax did not exist before 1913**; for over a century, the U.S. government primarily funded itself through **tariffs and excise taxes**, proving that an income tax is not a necessity for a functioning economy.
2. The **16th Amendment fundamentally altered the power dynamic** between the government and the American people, allowing an intrusive system that penalizes productivity and empowers politicians to manipulate taxpayers.
3. The **U.S. tax code spans over 70,000 pages**, an overly complex system riddled with loopholes that allow the ultra-wealthy and multinational corporations to exploit advantages unavailable to the average citizen.
4. **Middle-class workers and small businesses bear the brunt of taxation**, while many large corporations and wealthy elites use tax shelters, deductions, and offshore accounts to minimize their liabilities.
5. An estimated **40% of Americans pay no federal income tax**, yet they **vote on policies that redistribute wealth**, effectively allowing non-contributors to influence taxation and spending decisions.

Proposed Tax Reform

1. The Trump administration proposes **abolishing the income tax altogether** and eliminating the IRS as it currently operates, reducing federal overreach into personal finances.
2. **A Value-Added Tax (VAT) system** would replace income taxes, ensuring that every American contributes fairly through consumption-based taxation rather than penalizing earned income.
3. VAT taxes **spending instead of earnings**, incentivizing responsible saving and investment while discouraging excessive consumption without burdening job creation.
4. Because VAT is **collected at the point of sale**, it is significantly harder to evade, unlike income taxes that rely on self-reporting and extensive bureaucratic enforcement.
5. **A simplified tax system reduces administrative costs**, eliminating the need for millions of IRS agents and reducing government waste.

Alternative: Tariff-Based Revenue

1. Historically, the **U.S. government was almost entirely funded by tariffs**, and returning to a tariff-based system could reduce the need for direct taxation on citizens.
2. However, tariffs alone may not generate enough revenue without **massive government spending cuts**, which must be pursued in tandem with tax reform efforts.

Benefits of a VAT System Over Income Tax

1. **Encourages economic growth** by removing penalties on higher earnings.
2. **Simplifies tax collection**, reducing fraud and costly audits.
3. **Removes the IRS's ability to target individuals** based on political affiliation or financial status.
4. **Eliminates loopholes and deductions**, creating a fairer system.
5. **Protects the middle class**, as taxation is based on spending rather than arbitrary income brackets.

Challenges in Implementation

1. The transition will require **gradual reductions in income tax while phasing in VAT**, ensuring a smooth economic adjustment.
2. **Politicians and bureaucrats will resist**, as they benefit from the current system's complexity and the leverage it provides over taxpayers.
3. The **public may initially misunderstand VAT**, fearing it as an additional tax rather than a replacement for income tax.

....

CHAPTER 3: TERM LIMITS

The Dangers of Career Politicians

1. The **Founding Fathers never intended** for public service to become a lifelong career; they envisioned **citizen leadership**, where individuals served temporarily and then returned to private life.
2. **George Washington refused to seek a third term**, setting the precedent that leaders should not remain in power indefinitely.
3. **Congress has an 18% approval rating**, yet incumbents have a **90% re-election rate**, proving that elections alone do not remove

ineffective or corrupt politicians.

4. **Name recognition and media coverage** give incumbents a built-in advantage over challengers, discouraging competitive elections.
5. **Gerrymandering allows politicians to choose their voters**, securing safe districts that prevent real political accountability.

Corruption and Influence

1. **Long-term politicians build extensive donor networks**, making them dependent on **special interest groups and lobbyists** rather than their constituents.
2. **Lobbyists wield significant influence**, knowing that career politicians will prioritize campaign funding over genuine reform.
3. **Many members of Congress leave office far wealthier** than when they entered, raising concerns about insider trading and backdoor deals.
4. **Congress enjoys privileges the average American doesn't**, including **exclusive healthcare, high salaries, and generous pensions**, while many citizens struggle financially.
5. **Endless re-election cycles create a permanent campaign culture**, where politicians focus on fundraising rather than governance.

Proposed Term Limit Reform

1. **House of Representatives:** Maximum **12 years** (6 terms), ensuring fresh perspectives while maintaining experience.
2. **Senate:** Maximum **12 years** (2 terms), preventing political stagnation and entrenched power structures.
3. **Reduce congressional pensions**, stopping politicians from **retiring rich off taxpayer dollars** after decades in office.
4. **Grandfather in current members**, allowing term limits to take effect **without forcing immediate resignations**, which increases legislative support for the amendment.
5. Require **at least a 5-year gap** before former members of Congress can work as **lobbyists**, closing the revolving door between government and corporate interests.

Benefits of Term Limits

1. **New ideas and perspectives** will emerge as entrenched politicians are phased out.
2. **Reduces lobbyist control**, as politicians won't stay in office long

enough to develop deep financial ties.

3. **Politicians will focus on governance**, not just re-election strategies.
4. **Limits the accumulation of power**, preventing individuals from using decades in office to build unchecked influence.
5. **Increases accountability**, as lawmakers will no longer view Congress as a lifelong career.
6. **Encourages diverse candidates to run**, breaking the cycle of entrenched political dynasties.
7. Prevents **generational power hoarding**, where families treat public office as a hereditary right.

....

Chapter 4: A Balanced Budget Amendment

The National Debt Crisis

1. The **U.S. national debt exceeds $36 trillion**, a **financial catastrophe waiting to happen** if unchecked.
2. **The debt grows by $1 trillion every 100 days**, an unsustainable trajectory that threatens the country's economic future.
3. Congress has no incentive to stop reckless spending because **they won't personally face the consequences**—future generations will.
4. **49 out of 50 states are legally required to balance their budgets**, proving that it is possible to operate without endless deficit spending.
5. The federal government's ability to print money has **enabled inflation and devalued the dollar**, making everyday life more expensive for working Americans.

Arguments Against a Balanced Budget (and Why They're Wrong)

1. **"We need deficit spending for emergencies."**
   - **Solution:** Allow deficit spending only with a **supermajority vote**, ensuring it is used **only in genuine crises**.

2. **"It would force cuts to essential programs like Social Security and Medicare."**
   - **Solution:** Implement **gradual entitlement reforms** while cutting unnecessary programs, ensuring a **sustainable transition**.

3. **"A balanced budget would limit economic flexibility."**
   - ♦ **Solution:** Introduce **economic triggers** that allow temporary deficit spending **only during recessions.**

Path Forward for Implementation

1. **Public pressure is essential,** as polling shows that the majority of Americans support a **Balanced Budget Amendment.**
2. **Introduce the amendment gradually,** preventing economic shocks by phasing in spending limits over time.
3. **Require Congress to justify new spending,** making it harder for politicians to pass wasteful bills without accountability.
4. **Cap federal spending at a fixed percentage of GDP,** preventing reckless borrowing.
5. **End baseline budgeting,** which automatically increases government spending each year without justification.

Long-Term Impact of a Balanced Budget Amendment

1. Forces Congress to **prioritize spending,** rather than constantly increasing the national debt.
2. **Reduces government expansion,** limiting unnecessary federal agencies and regulatory overreach.
3. **Restores economic stability,** making the U.S. a safer investment for businesses and international markets.
4. **Stops excessive taxation,** as the government will no longer rely on increased revenue to cover its spending habits.
5. **Reduces inflation,** as the government will be unable to flood the economy with newly printed money.
6. **Encourages responsible financial policies,** ensuring that the government operates within its means.
7. **Protects future generations from financial collapse,** preventing a situation where national debt leads to economic disaster.

CHAPTER 5: ZERO-BASE BUDGETING – A PATH TO FISCAL RESPONSIBILITY

Understanding Zero-Base Budgeting (ZBB)

1. **Zero-base budgeting (ZBB)** requires every department to justify all expenses **starting from zero** each budget cycle, rather than adjusting from previous budgets.
2. Unlike traditional budgeting, which assumes prior expenditures as the baseline, ZBB forces **every dollar to be accounted for and justified.**
3. Departments must **evaluate spending priorities** rather than relying on automatic budget increases.
4. **The process involves:**
    *   Identifying **decision units** (departments, agencies, programs).

    *   Presenting **cost-effective alternatives** (bare minimum to optimal funding levels).

    *   **Ranking priorities** to allocate resources efficiently.

5. Originally developed for the **private sector** by Peter Pyhrr at Texas Instruments, ZBB has been proposed as a tool for **public financial reform.**

The Case for Zero-Base Budgeting

1. **Eliminates wasteful spending** by identifying unnecessary or outdated programs that continue to receive funding.
2. Forces **every department to justify its budget,** increasing **accountability and transparency.**
3. **Flexibility and adaptability** allow for quick reallocation of resources during **national emergencies or economic shifts.**
4. Discourages **"use-it-or-lose-it" spending,** where departments rush to spend remaining funds at the end of the fiscal year.
5. Encourages **long-term financial planning** by ensuring funding is aligned with actual needs and national priorities.

Criticisms of Zero-Base Budgeting

1. Critics argue that ZBB is **resource-intensive**, requiring extensive data collection and justification.
2. **Bureaucratic resistance** is a concern, as agencies accustomed to automatic increases may resist scrutiny.
3. Some worry about **over-simplification**, where certain programs may not show immediate returns but have long-term benefits.
4. **Short-term vs. long-term focus:** ZBB must be structured to ensure long-term investments (infrastructure, research) are not neglected.

Why Zero-Base Budgeting is Necessary Today

1. The **U.S. national debt exceeds $36 trillion,** necessitating immediate fiscal discipline.
2. ZBB **aligns spending with national priorities,** ensuring outdated programs do not siphon funds from urgent needs.
3. By increasing **public transparency**, ZBB strengthens trust in government and **reduces fraud and mismanagement.**
4. **Implementing Zero-Base Budgeting in Phases**
5. A **phased rollout** would start with discretionary spending and expand to all federal agencies.
6. **Leveraging technology** would streamline data analysis and budget justification processes.
7. Encouraging a **culture shift** in government agencies toward fiscal responsibility is critical for success.

Final Thoughts

1. Traditional budgeting **fuels reckless spending** and **enables wasteful government growth**—ZBB provides a **much-needed course correction.**
2. While not a cure-all, ZBB is a **powerful tool** that can help steer America toward financial sustainability.

Chapter 6: Election Integrity – Securing Democracy Through Common-Sense Reforms

Concerns Over Election Integrity

1. Public confidence in elections has declined due to **widespread concerns about fraud, transparency, and accountability.**
2. The **expansion of mail-in voting in 2020** raised security risks, including ballot harvesting and inaccurate voter rolls.
3. The film **2000 Mules** raised questions about potential election fraud, particularly regarding ballot drop boxes.
4. **Three Key Election Integrity Reforms**
5. **1. Voter ID: A Common-Sense Safeguard**
6. **Voter ID ensures only eligible citizens vote**, preventing impersonation and duplicate ballots.
7. Critics argue that voter ID laws **disenfranchise vulnerable populations**, but IDs are required for many daily activities.
8. **Free or low-cost IDs** can be provided to eliminate accessibility concerns.
9. **Most developed nations** require voter ID, proving it is a standard security measure.
10. **2. Paper Ballots: The Gold Standard of Accountability**
11. **Electronic voting machines are vulnerable to hacking and technical failures.**
12. **Paper ballots provide a verifiable, physical audit trail**, reducing the risk of election tampering.
13. Hand-counting ballots may take longer, but **accuracy should be prioritized over speed.**
14. **3. Election Day as a National Holiday, Limited to One Day of Voting**
15. Extending voting over **weeks creates security vulnerabilities** and opportunities for manipulation.
16. Making **Election Day a national holiday** ensures more citizens can participate without work-related conflicts.
17. A **single voting day enhances trust in the process** by ensuring all ballots are cast under the same conditions.
18. **Final Thoughts**
19. Implementing these three reforms will **restore faith in American elections** and ensure every legal vote counts.
20. **Election integrity is non-partisan**—a secure voting system benefits all Americans, regardless of political affiliation.

CHAPTER 7: REDUCING THE ADMINISTRATIVE STATE – RESTORING POWER TO THE PEOPLE

The Problem of Government Overgrowth

1. The **federal bureaucracy has ballooned**, creating inefficiency, waste, and **lack of accountability.**
2. Many federal agencies operate **outside the oversight of elected officials**, making policy decisions without public input.
3. **Duplication and redundancy** across agencies contribute to massive budget waste.
4. **Proposed Reforms to Reduce Bureaucracy**
5. **Cut the federal workforce by 75%** to eliminate redundant positions and streamline operations.
6. **Shift responsibilities to state and local governments**, reducing unnecessary federal oversight.
7. **Consolidate overlapping agencies**, preventing duplication of services and reducing costs.
8. **Leverage technology** to automate government functions, improving efficiency.
9. **Deregulate industries** by removing outdated rules that stifle economic growth.
10. **Restoring Accountability**
11. The **power of unelected bureaucrats** must be curtailed by returning authority to **elected officials.**
12. **Congress must reclaim its legislative role**, rather than outsourcing policymaking to federal agencies.
13. Regulatory reform should be focused on **cutting unnecessary red tape** while maintaining essential protections.
14. **Final Thoughts**
15. The administrative state is an **obstacle to democracy**, expanding government control beyond its constitutional limits.
16. Shrinking the federal bureaucracy will **restore power to the people** and **enhance government efficiency.**

CHAPTER 8: MERIT VS. DEI – THE FIGHT FOR FAIRNESS AND EXCELLENCE

The Rise of DEI and Its Impact

1. Diversity, Equity, and Inclusion (DEI) policies aim to **address past discrimination**, but often **undermine merit-based systems.**

2. **Hiring, admissions, and promotions based on identity rather than achievement** lead to inefficiency and resentment.
3. Many companies are now **abandoning DEI programs** due to legal challenges and public backlash.

Why Merit Matters

1. **Meritocracy rewards hard work, talent, and innovation**, ensuring the most qualified individuals succeed.
2. **Identity-based hiring and education lower standards**, prioritizing demographics over competence.
3. The **U.S. Supreme Court's 2023 ruling against affirmative action** reaffirmed the importance of merit in college admissions.

DEI in the Military and Public Sector

1. The **military's DEI initiatives have weakened combat readiness**, prioritizing diversity over performance.
2. **Government hiring preferences based on race and gender** distort competition and efficiency.
3. DEI has **fueled division and resentment** rather than fostering true inclusion.
4. **Fixing the System: A Merit-Based Alternative**
5. Implement **blind recruitment and promotion processes** to ensure fairness.
6. Shift from **identity-based programs** to **socioeconomic support**, helping all disadvantaged individuals.
7. **Prioritize skills and experience** over race or gender in hiring and admissions.
8. **Final Thoughts**
9. **DEI policies have outlived their usefulness**, creating more division than opportunity.
10. A return to **merit-based systems will restore excellence, fairness, and national unity.**

Chapter 9: Freedom of Speech

1. **First Amendment Protection** – The U.S. Constitution guarantees freedom of speech by prohibiting government suppression of expression. However, this right does not extend to private entities, meaning social media companies and corporations can impose their own speech restrictions.

2. **Limitations on Speech** – While free speech is broad, the Supreme Court has ruled that certain forms, such as incitement to violence, defamation, and threats, are not protected under the First Amendment and can be legally restricted.

3. **Content Neutrality** – The government cannot restrict speech based on its content unless the law serves a compelling interest and is narrowly tailored. Any attempts to silence speech must pass strict legal scrutiny.

4. **Public vs. Private Regulation** – The First Amendment prevents government interference in speech but does not apply to private businesses, meaning platforms like Twitter, Facebook, and YouTube can moderate content as they see fit.

5. **Symbolic Speech** – Nonverbal forms of expression, such as burning the American flag or kneeling during the national anthem, have been ruled as protected speech under the First Amendment, further expanding its reach.

6. **Censorship Concerns** – Many individuals, including the author, have faced censorship, shadow-banning, and suppression of their work on social media platforms simply for expressing viewpoints that challenge mainstream narratives.

7. **Section 230 Protection** – This provision of the Communications Decency Act shields online platforms from liability for user-generated content, allowing them to moderate without being legally considered publishers.

8. **Moderation vs. Censorship** – Section 230 enables social media companies to remove content they deem objectionable without losing legal protections, creating a gray area between fair moderation and political censorship.

9. **Criticism of Section 230** – Many argue that this law grants tech companies too much power, allowing them to shape public discourse while remaining unaccountable for biased enforcement of their policies.

10. **Biden Administration and Amazon** – Reports have surfaced that the Biden administration pressured Amazon to suppress books skeptical of COVID-19 vaccines, raising concerns over government influence on private companies.

11. **Government Influence Over Free Speech** – Allegedly, at least 43 books were targeted for censorship, including the author's own publications, highlighting the extent of federal pressure on private entities.

12. **Censorship of "Fauci's Fiction"** – The author's book, which analyzed COVID-19 data, faced advertising bans and suppression, limiting its visibility despite widespread praise for its research.

13. **YouTube Deplatforming** – After an interview with vaccine injury advocate Brianne Dressen, YouTube permanently banned the

author's channel, citing "medical misinformation," despite the discussion being fact-based.

14. **The Cost of Speaking Out** – Content creators risk being demonetized, banned, or deplatformed if they voice opinions that contradict prevailing narratives on topics like vaccines, elections, or government policies.

15. **Algorithms as Tools of Control** – Social media algorithms are designed to suppress or promote certain content, giving tech companies the ability to subtly manipulate what people see and believe.

16. **The Chilling Effect** – Fear of censorship discourages open discussion, leading many content creators to self-censor and avoid controversial topics altogether.

17. **The Role of Big Tech in Speech Regulation** – Major digital platforms have become the dominant public square, yet their unchecked control over speech raises serious questions about free expression in the digital age.

18. **Lack of Legal Recourse** – Defending free speech in court is costly, meaning only those with significant financial resources can challenge censorship effectively.

19. **Government Overreach Must Be Stopped** – Federal and corporate collaboration to suppress dissenting voices is a direct attack on First Amendment values and should be opposed at all levels.

20. **Defending Free Speech is Essential** – If the fundamental right to free speech is lost, all other freedoms will follow, making it imperative to push back against censorship and protect open dialogue.

CHAPTER 10: DIGITAL CURRENCY AND GOVERNMENT CONTROL

1. **Origins of Digital Currency** – While digital transactions have existed for decades, Bitcoin's creation in 2009 revolutionized the concept of decentralized, government-free money.

2. **Bitcoin's Impact** – Bitcoin was designed as an alternative to traditional banking, allowing peer-to-peer transactions that bypass government control and financial institutions.

3. **Rise of Central Bank Digital Currencies (CBDCs)** – Many governments now seek to create their own digital currencies, but unlike Bitcoin, these are fully controlled and monitored by the state.

4. **China's Digital Yuan** – China's CBDC allows real-time surveillance of transactions, enabling the Communist Party to enforce compliance and punish dissent through financial restrictions.

5. **Sweden's e-Krona** – While promoted as a convenient digital alternative to cash, Sweden's push toward a cashless society raises concerns about excluding those without digital access.

6. **Bahamas' Sand Dollar** – A small-scale experiment in digital currency aimed at improving financial inclusion, though its adoption remains limited.

7. **Erosion of Financial Privacy** – Unlike cash, digital currency leaves a permanent, traceable record of every transaction, allowing the government to monitor and potentially control personal finances.

8. **CBDCs as a Control Tool** – Governments could program digital currency to limit spending, impose expiration dates on funds, or block purchases of politically disfavored goods and services.

9. **Expiration of Funds** – A central bank could force consumers to spend money within a set period, reducing personal financial autonomy.

10. **Banning Certain Purchases** – A CBDC system could prevent users from buying items deemed "unnecessary" or "harmful" by the government.

11. **Seizing Digital Assets** – With centralized control, governments could freeze or confiscate funds at will, bypassing traditional legal processes.

12. **Cybersecurity Risks** – A CBDC system creates a single point of failure, making it a prime target for hackers who could disrupt the economy.

13. **Disrupting Financial Institutions** – Widespread adoption of CBDCs could reduce the role of private banks, limiting access to credit and destabilizing traditional banking systems.

14. **Exclusion of Vulnerable Populations** – A fully digital economy could leave behind the elderly, rural populations, and those without reliable internet access.

15. **Elimination of Cash Risks Economic Stability** – Relying solely on digital currency removes the backup option of cash transactions during power outages or cyberattacks.

16. **Lessons from History** – Governments have a track record of using financial systems to suppress political opposition and dissent.

17. **Opposition to CBDCs** – Many experts argue that digital currencies should remain decentralized and free from government intervention to prevent financial oppression.

18. **Existing Alternatives** – Private-sector innovations like cryptocurrencies and fintech solutions already provide fast, low-cost digital transactions without requiring government control.

19. **The Path Forward** – A balanced approach that preserves financial freedom while addressing fraud and efficiency concerns is preferable to full government control of currency.

20. **Keeping Government Out of Your Wallet** – Resisting CBDCs is critical to ensuring that financial autonomy and individual rights remain protected from government overreach.

Chapter 11: Eliminate the Department of Education

1. **The Department of Education (ED) was established in 1980** – Initially created to improve educational outcomes, it has instead led to increased bureaucracy and federal overreach.
2. **The Constitution does not grant the federal government authority over education** – Under the Tenth Amendment, education is supposed to be managed by states and local communities, not Washington, D.C.
3. **The Department of Education has a $241 billion budget** – Despite this massive spending, educational outcomes in the U.S. have stagnated, and American students continue to fall behind internationally.
4. **Bureaucratic waste consumes funding** – A significant portion of the DOE's budget is spent on administrative costs rather than directly benefiting students and teachers.
5. **Federal education mandates harm local schools** – Programs like No Child Left Behind and Common Core have imposed top-down regulations that prioritize compliance over quality education.
6. **Standardized testing has failed students** – Schools teach to pass the test rather than fostering critical thinking, creativity, or vocational skills.
7. **Parental rights are being eroded** – Federal education policies increasingly push ideological agendas that limit parental control over what their children learn.
8. **Education funding should remain at the state and local level** – Local governments are better equipped to allocate resources based on the unique needs of their communities.
9. **School choice improves education** – Charter schools, voucher programs, and homeschooling allow competition, which drives better outcomes for students.
10. **Eliminating the DOE would empower teachers** – Removing federal oversight would allow educators to focus on teaching rather than bureaucratic mandates.
11. **The DOE prioritizes political agendas over education** – Federal education initiatives often push ideological policies instead of focusing on academic excellence.
12. **Special interests and teachers' unions control federal education policy** – These groups often prioritize job security and funding over student achievement.
13. **Government involvement in student loans has inflated tuition** – Federal student loan programs have driven up college costs by providing institutions with guaranteed funding.

14. **Decentralizing education leads to innovation** – When states control their education policies, they can tailor programs to their students' needs rather than following one-size-fits-all federal mandates.

15. **Eliminating the DOE would reduce federal spending** – Taxpayers would save billions annually if education funding were handled more efficiently at the state level.

16. **Education decisions should be in the hands of families** – Parents, not bureaucrats, should have the ultimate authority over their children's education.

17. **Abolishing the DOE would not harm disadvantaged students** – States would still receive federal block grants to support low-income and special-needs students.

18. **Higher education should not be federally controlled** – College admissions, curricula, and financial aid should be determined by individual institutions and state governments, not federal regulators.

19. **Teachers' unions resist education reform** – Many unions prioritize job protection over meaningful improvements in education quality.

20. **Returning education to the states is the only way to restore accountability** – Eliminating the Department of Education would put power back in the hands of local communities and improve educational outcomes.

CHAPTER 12: UNION INFLUENCE

1. **Unions originally formed to protect workers** – In the 19th and early 20th centuries, unions helped improve wages, working conditions, and labor laws.

2. **Most worker protections are now covered by law** – Laws such as the Fair Labor Standards Act, OSHA, and anti-discrimination laws have reduced the need for unions.

3. **Unions can impose financial burdens on businesses** – Higher wages, pensions, and restrictive work rules make it difficult for companies to stay competitive.

4. **Union strikes disrupt industries** – Work stoppages in sectors like manufacturing, education, and transportation often harm consumers and the economy.

5. **Public-sector unions burden taxpayers** – Government employee unions negotiate generous benefits, often leading to underfunded pensions and higher taxes.

6. **Unions resist merit-based pay** – Instead of rewarding the best workers, unions often prioritize seniority, making it difficult to remove underperforming employees.

7. **Teachers' unions hinder education reform** – They frequently oppose school choice, charter schools, and curriculum improvements to protect their influence.

8. **Unions oppose automation and modernization** – In industries like auto manufacturing, union resistance to innovation has hurt competitiveness.

9. **Corruption is rampant in major unions** – Many high-profile union leaders have been caught embezzling funds or engaging in self-serving practices.

10. **Unions contribute to higher consumer prices** – Increased labor costs are often passed down to customers, raising prices on goods and services.

11. **Government unions negotiate against taxpayers** – Unlike private-sector unions, public-sector unions bargain with politicians who use taxpayer money, creating conflicts of interest.

12. **Union membership has declined significantly** – Many workers now see unions as outdated or unnecessary in the modern workforce.

13. **Forced union dues violate worker choice** – Many states require workers to pay union dues even if they do not want to be part of a union.

14. **Unions fund political agendas** – Many unions use member dues to support political causes, often against the interests of the workers they claim to represent.

15. **Right-to-work laws give employees more freedom** – In states with these laws, workers are not forced to join unions or pay dues to keep their jobs.

16. **Union pension liabilities are unsustainable** – Many states and municipalities face massive pension shortfalls due to overly generous union contracts.

17. **Unions block business growth** – Excessive regulations and labor demands discourage companies from expanding or hiring more workers.

18. **Unionized workplaces have rigid rules** – Companies struggle to adjust staffing levels, schedules, and policies due to restrictive union contracts.

19. **Unions protect incompetent employees** – It is often nearly impossible to fire bad workers in unionized workplaces, lowering overall productivity.

20. **Modern workplaces require flexibility, not union control** – Today's economy demands innovation and adaptability, which are often stifled by rigid union rules.

CHAPTER 13: IT'S ALL ABOUT THE ENERGY
(BUT MOSTLY MONEY AND POWER)

1. **Energy is the foundation of the economy** – Every aspect of economic stability, from inflation to job growth, is tied to energy availability and affordability.
2. **The U.S. has abundant fossil fuel reserves** – America possesses large quantities of oil, natural gas, and coal, yet restrictive policies limit their full utilization.
3. **America's coal reserves are among the largest in the world** – The U.S. holds about 25-30% of the world's recoverable coal reserves, providing a significant energy security buffer.
4. **Fossil fuels remain critical to national security** – Reducing reliance on domestic oil and gas weakens the economy and makes the U.S. more dependent on foreign nations.
5. **Green energy policies are driven by ideology, not economics** – Many progressive climate policies prioritize political narratives over economic realities.
6. **Renewable energy is unreliable** – Wind and solar power face intermittency issues, requiring fossil fuel backups to maintain grid stability.
7. **Infrastructure costs for renewables are enormous** – Transitioning fully to green energy would require trillions in government spending and taxpayer funding.
8. **China and India are the real polluters** – While the U.S. is pushed to adopt costly climate policies, nations like China and India continue expanding coal and fossil fuel use.
9. **Government regulations artificially raise energy prices** – Restrictions on drilling, pipeline construction, and refining have directly contributed to higher fuel and electricity costs.
10. **The push to eliminate fossil fuels is unrealistic** – Even the most optimistic projections show that fossil fuels will still be necessary for decades.
11. **Energy independence reduces inflation** – Under Trump, increased domestic production lowered energy prices, benefiting consumers and businesses alike.
12. **The Biden administration's policies have hurt energy production** – The cancellation of pipelines, leasing restrictions, and regulatory burdens have led to price spikes.
13. **Nuclear energy is a better alternative than wind and solar** – It provides reliable, zero-carbon power but is opposed by many of the same environmental activists who push green energy.
14. **The media distorts energy policy debates** – Left-leaning outlets

frame fossil fuels as inherently bad while ignoring the shortcomings of renewables.

15. **Climate change is used as a political weapon** – Many proposed policies do little to address environmental concerns but expand government power over industry.

16. **Extreme weather events are falsely blamed on fossil fuels** – Every hurricane, wildfire, and drought is used as a justification for costly climate initiatives.

17. **Energy policies should prioritize economic stability** – The primary goal should be ensuring affordable energy for all Americans, not virtue signaling to global elites.

18. **Green energy subsidies benefit large corporations** – Taxpayer money is funneled into politically connected companies while small businesses and consumers bear the costs.

19. **Trump understands the importance of energy dominance** – His policies focused on strengthening America's energy sector rather than weakening it through regulation.

20. **Energy policy should be dictated by facts, not fear** – The U.S. should pursue a balanced approach, utilizing all available energy sources to maintain economic strength.

Chapter 14: Déjà Vu

1. **America has been facing the same problems for decades** – Many of today's political debates were already being addressed in the 1990s under the Contract with America.

2. **The Contract with America was a Republican reform plan** – In 1994, Newt Gingrich led an effort to restore fiscal responsibility, shrink government, and strengthen national security.

3. **The plan emphasized a balanced budget** – Republicans pushed for a constitutional amendment requiring the federal government to live within its means.

4. **Crime reduction was a major priority** – The proposal called for more law enforcement funding, stricter sentencing, and prison expansion.

5. **Welfare reform was a key issue** – Republicans sought to reduce dependency by implementing work requirements and limiting benefits.

6. **Tax cuts were central to the plan** – The GOP pushed for reductions in taxes and a simplified tax code to stimulate economic growth.

7. **Term limits were proposed but never enacted** – A major failure of the movement was the inability to pass congressional term limits.

8. **Many of these reforms were temporary fixes** – While some policies had short-term success, long-term structural changes were not made.
9. **The problems of today mirror those of the past** – High inflation, illegal immigration, and government overspending remain major concerns.
10. **The media played a similar role then and now** – The press worked to undermine Republican efforts in the 1990s, just as they attack conservative policies today.
11. **Swing voters dictate political shifts** – Moderate and independent voters determine the direction of the country based on economic conditions.
12. **The Biden administration has mirrored past Democratic failures** – Open borders, reckless spending, and economic mismanagement have led to predictable outcomes.
13. **Leftist policies ignore basic economics** – Progressive taxation, climate initiatives, and social spending consistently lead to stagnation.
14. **Crime and immigration are worsening under liberal governance** – Cities run by Democrats have seen increases in crime, homelessness, and illegal immigration.
15. **The left refuses to address real concerns** – Progressive leaders focus on identity politics and social justice rather than economic stability.
16. **The political pendulum always swings back** – When Democrats overreach, voters return to conservative policies to restore order.
17. **Trump's policies resonate with the majority** – His economic and national security agenda aligns with what most Americans want.
18. **The media distorts Trump's success** – They portray his policies as radical, despite their widespread popularity among voters.
19. **America has one opportunity to enact real change** – If the Trump administration doesn't pass lasting reforms, future Democrats will undo progress.
20. **We must act decisively to save the country** – Half-measures won't work—deep structural reforms are needed to preserve America's future.

....

CHAPTER 15: ONE CHANCE FOR THE REPUBLIC

1. **Trump's return has reinvigorated conservatives - His second administration has a clear focus:** reversing the damage of the Biden years.

2. **The administration is operating at high speed** – Rapid policy roll-outs prevent Democrats from effectively mounting opposition.
3. **The left's response is predictable** – They delay appointments, obstruct legislation, and use legal challenges to slow progress.
4. **Media deception is at an all-time high** – News outlets fabricate controversies to distract from Trump's policy achievements.
5. **Progressives don't understand what they oppose** – Many leftists criticize conservatism without comprehending its core principles.
6. **Social media amplifies misinformation** – False narratives spread quickly, shaping public perception in ways that distort reality.
7. **Elon Musk's exposure of government waste is significant** – His efforts to reveal corruption in Washington threaten the establishment.
8. **Bureaucrats wield enormous unchecked power** – Unelected officials control much of the government with little accountability.
9. **The left thrives on manufactured outrage** – They rely on crisis narratives to justify expanding government control.
10. **Debating progressives is often futile** – They use emotional appeals rather than logical arguments to push their agenda.
11. **Trump's political break strengthened him** – His time away from office gave him a clearer strategy for long-term success.
12. **Democrats oppose conservative policies regardless of merit** – Even when reforms help the country, the left resists purely out of partisanship.
13. **Permanent policy changes must be enacted** – Temporary victories will be undone by future leftist administrations.
14. **Border security is a non-negotiable priority** – Without strict immigration enforcement, national sovereignty is at risk.
15. **Government overreach is eroding personal freedom** – Regulations, taxation, and censorship continue to grow unchecked.
16. **The silent majority supports conservative reforms** – Despite media portrayals, most Americans back Trump's policies.
17. **This is a once-in-a-lifetime opportunity** – If conservatives fail to act, America may never recover from its decline.
18. **Trump's policies benefit all Americans** – His focus on economic growth, national security, and freedom helps the entire country.
19. **The left's resistance is about control, not progress** – They fear losing power more than they care about actual policy outcomes.
20. **We must fight to save America** – This administration represents the last real chance to restore the republic before it's too late.

Acknowledgements

To my wife, Kelly—your love and patience mean everything. Without you, I wouldn't have accomplished half of what I have.

Jaiden, I love you and admire everything you've become. Whether you choose to be a lawyer, lobbyist, or anything else your heart desires, I know you'll excel. Stay positive and keep moving forward.

Vincent, you are the best writing companion. You've gone three for three—get ready for the next project, and don't worry, the treats will be waiting!

To my assistant Caitlin, my staff, and all our part-timers, interns, and students, past and present—you are valued more than you may realize.

To the ones who keep me sane and embody the true meaning of "family"—Pat Conway, Jeannie Conway, Jess Lange, Donnie McCrickard, Gianna, and Ryder—I love and appreciate you.

A special thank you to my mother Judy, my father Joe, Paul Rotella, Phil Perricone, Marilyn Perricone, Mike Caldarise, Terry Condio, Nick Naumoff, and everyone at Rumble. To the best publicist in the world, Stacy Sutphen at Part Time Hero Productions—you rock!

To all the fans of *The Mike Schwartz Show* and *2 Mikes Live*, especially our chat—you amaze me every day with your support. It still blows my mind that you tune in daily to hear what I have to say!

To Carnella and Joe—thank you for your wisdom and guidance. We miss you.

To my Bats brothers, the NY Yankees, my sister, brother in law and nieces and nephew, Laura Coreas, Tony Coreas, Larissa Coreas, Fredys Coreas, Victoria Coreas, and Amada Coreas—thank you.

A heartfelt thank you to Amber May Hilliker, Jeff Ahern, Isaac Hayes, the Bearded Viking Mead Boys, JT, Rudy, Alex, Dan Nunn, Wendy Mitchell and all the other warriors fighting to tell the TRUTH!

And to one of my best friends in life, Juan Bellu. Losing you this year was heartbreaking. After 25 years of friendship—flying planes, Civil Air Patrol, rotary meetings, holidays, vacations, and countless conversations—you were more than a friend, you were a mentor. When I stepped into politics, you took me under your wing, teaching me lessons I didn't even know I needed. You will be missed more than words can express.

About the Author

Dr. Michael J. Schwartz has been a dedicated entrepreneur since 1993. He holds a Doctorate in Business Administration along with numerous degrees, licenses, and certifications. His political career began at a young age, and he has served as a senior advisor to multiple candidates. Schwartz is a bestselling author of *Fauci's Fiction* and *Vaccine Fiction*. His dissertation, housed in the Library of Congress, explores the impact of the CARES Act on COVID-19 testing and treatment.

Throughout his career, Schwartz has owned and operated a wide range of businesses, including multiple medical clinics and a consulting firm specializing in educating physicians and practitioners on genetics and respiratory pathogens in immunology. A former police officer, he is also an accomplished private pilot and a devoted New York Yankees fan.

Schwartz developed and taught *The Secrets of Body Language and Communication*, a course presented to both private and governmental organizations. He has been performing stand-up comedy since his early 20s and remains an active performer. A familiar face on television and radio, he hosts *The Mike Schwartz Show* and co-hosts *2 Mikes Live* on Rumble. His work has been featured in *Newsweek* and *All Sides*.

In 2008, Schwartz founded the charity Hometown Heroes, which has distributed millions of dollars to those in need. The organization has earned widespread recognition, including the prestigious Robin Hood Service Award. He has served on numerous boards and received various distinguished accolades for his business achievements and philanthropy. Schwartz is a recipient of the Paul Harris Fellow from Rotary International and has been honored by the United Way with their *Top 40 Under 40* award. During his time as a police officer, he was decorated with both a Class A and Class C Meritorious Service Award.

Schwartz divides his time between Wall, New Jersey, and Tampa, Florida.